Strategic Marketing Planning for the Small to Medium-Sized Business

Strategic Marketing Planning for the Small to Medium-Sized Business

Writing a Marketing Plan

David W. Anderson

Strategic Marketing Planning for the Small to Medium-Sized Business:
Writing a Marketing Plan
Copyright © Business Expert Press, LLC, 2012.

First published in 2012 by
Business Expert Press, LLC
222 East 46th Street, New York, NY 10017
www.businessexpertpress.com

ISBN-13: 978-1-60649-373-1 (paperback)
ISBN-13: 978-1-60649-374-8 (e-book)

DOI 10.4128/ 9781606493748

A publication in the Business Expert Press Marketing Strategy collection

Collection ISSN: 2150-9654 (print)
Collection ISSN: 2150-9662 (electronic)

Cover design by Jonathan Pennell
Interior design by Scribe Inc.

First edition: January 2012

10 9 8 7 6 5 4 3 2 1

Printed in the United States of America.

Abstract

Regrettably, 80% of small to medium-sized businesses fail within 2 years of their inception. Ninety percent of businesses close after 10 years of operation. Although there may be many reasons, the lack of a strategic, actionable, and measurable marketing plan is often the underlying cause.

Marketing a business in today's extremely competitive marketplace is difficult at best. Money is tight. Customers are more demanding. Moreover, the vast array of strategic and promotional alternatives available to business owners and marketers can be perplexing, confusing, and frustrating.

Based on 30 years of experience in domestic and international business-to-business and consumer marketing, this book is an excellent marketing development tool for the small to medium-sized business.

Creating a strategic marketing plan for your business may appear to be a daunting task. Indeed, many business owners simply don't do it. Others create a flawed plan because they lack an actionable and measurable process.

Strategic Marketing Planning for the Small to Medium-Sized Business addresses these issues by providing both marketing theory and workbook exercises. This book offers the small to medium-sized business owner or marketing staff a hands-on experience that will culminate in the development of a true marketing plan, specifically tailored to an individual business.

From developing or refining the company's mission, goals, and strategies to creating budgets and implementing tactics, this book provides the information and framework needed to develop a sound marketing plan that will help your business grow.

Keywords

Strategic marketing, marketing your small to medium-sized business, marketing planning, advertising planning, business planning, how to select media, setting goals, strategies and tactics, marketing measurement, marketing workbook, business planning, strategic planning, advertising and promotions, trade show marketing, company growth, how to market, creating your marketing plan

Contents

Acknowledgments

Publication of this book would not have been possible without Bruce Bishline, BS. Based on his years of experience in retail business, retail marketing, and business academics, Bruce tirelessly reviewed this book and provided valuable suggestions, objective viewpoints, and real-life insights. Bruce is an expert in small business start-ups as well as in growing existing businesses. He currently works in adult education at Tulsa Tech and conducts classes for entrepreneurs and business owners. I was extremely fortunate that Bruce was willing to share his time and expertise. Bruce's business blog is located at http://www.bishline.com.

From the Author

Regrettably, 80% of small to medium-sized businesses fail within 2 years of their inception. Ninety percent of businesses close after 10 years of operation. Although there may be many reasons, the lack of a strategic, actionable, and measurable marketing plan often is the underlying cause.

Marketing a business in today's extremely competitive marketplace is difficult, at best. Money is tight. Customers are more demanding. Moreover, the vast array of strategic and promotional alternatives available to business owners and marketers can be perplexing, confusing, and frustrating.

Based on 30 years of experience in domestic and international business-to-business and consumer marketing, this book is an excellent marketing development tool for the small to medium-sized business.

Creating a strategic marketing plan for your business may appear to be a daunting task. Indeed, many business owners simply don't do it. Others create a flawed plan because they lack an actionable and measurable process.

Strategic Marketing Planning for the Small to Medium-Sized Business addresses these issues by providing both marketing theory and workbook exercises. This book offers the small to medium-sized business owner or marketing staff a hands-on experience that will culminate in the development of a true marketing plan, specifically tailored to an individual business.

From developing or refining the company's mission, goals, and strategies to creating budgets and implementing tactics, this book provides the information and framework needed to develop a sound marketing plan that will help your business grow.

There are many books about the theories of marketing, but few include a hands-on implementation component. The purpose of this manual is to guide you through the jungle of marketing planning. By using this manual, you will be able to develop a plan specifically tailored to the needs of your business.

First, you will perform the necessary *research* on which you will base
    logical and sound business decisions.

Second, you will create a *mission statement* for your business, which will
    act as the guiding light throughout your marketing journey.

Third, you will develop the *goals, strategies, tactics, and budgets* that will
    form the infrastructure of your marketing plan.

Fourth, you will *integrate* the plan into your day-to-day routine so it will
    become "part of the woodwork."

Last, you will *measure* the success of your efforts and *modify* the plan as
    needed to continue with your success.

Throughout the years, marketers have experimented with many
types of marketing structures. This system of plan development is the
one that works.

We will offer you a word of caution. Although this book offers an
excellent *framework* for designing a marketing plan, the success of your
efforts will depend completely on the effort you put into it. *The plan will
not create itself!*

How to Use This Manual

Strategic Marketing Planning for the Small to Medium-Sized Business is designed for the business owner. It will generate many thoughts and ideas that are important to building your plan. We urge you to make notes, to read with a pencil in hand. Ask yourself questions as you go. If the manual presents options to you, circle the one that is most appropriate to your situation. It should be your goal to write notes or comments on every page.

In addition, this manual will often ask you questions or ask you to complete a form *before you have all the information you need*. Although this may strike you as odd, it is a way to begin the process that will allow you to discover what you are missing so that you can complete the element later. You will have many opportunities to return and complete the task. You also may find that you will need to return to certain sections of the book and modify your earlier thoughts. This has proven to be an effective method of self-study.

Once you have completed the book, you will be able to compile all the information you have gathered into a master document—one that you can actually use.

We hope you will take the opportunity to "plan your work and work your plan" using this manual as a guide. If you do, the results can be truly outstanding.

Best of luck to you!

David W. Anderson

CHAPTER 1

Marketing Theory

Real Life

Marketing begins at birth. As infants, we cry to receive attention. As we grow, we learn to negotiate for what we want using a variety of techniques, including tantrums, pleading, and the triangulation of parents as required.

Indeed, we have all been "selling" for most of our lives. We just do not think of it in those terms.

Marketing has been part of the human culture since the beginning of trade. Names once illustrated a person's craft. For example, the names "Tanner," "Fisher," "Sawyer," and "Skinner" once described a person's profession or area of proficiency. This was an excellent way for a prospective customer to identify the local blacksmith as well as for the blacksmith to advertise his services. Modern branding theory grew from this nomenclature system and is still in use today.

Tactically, signs and illustrations were among the first physical forms of advertising. Signs often displayed an image of the craft or service offered, as symbols were easily recognizable and literacy was scarce. Today, we still see the three spheres adorning the signs of pawnshops, but many of the other old icons have disappeared (although it is interesting to note that today's marketers are now returning to this type of iconic signage and branding, using a symbol without accompanying words).

During Shakespearean times, actors took to the streets to promote the local plays, and peddlers hawked their wares in the streets, stimulating trial via product sampling. Technological advances have changed marketing tactics, but the principles of applied behavioral change have remained much the same.

The formal field of advertising began in America when Volney B. Palmer opened an advertising agency in Philadelphia, Pennsylvania, in 1842.

Mass marketing began to develop around 1850 in America when the population had grown to an appropriate size and the necessary channels had developed. Newspapers provided a primary communications channel, and advertising "systems" began to appear, offering rudimentary planning and creative services versus simply offering space in newspapers.

In the 1950s, advertising agencies began to flourish and colleges began to explore management and marketing theories. This led to the "Mad men" of advertising agencies in the 1960s and the employment of management theories of "management by objectives," which was a thrilling new concept at the time. The industry continued to grow and to refine advertising in terms of unique selling propositions and limited database marketing. However, agencies continued to focus on advertising, leaving marketing to their clients. By the 1990s, the *relationship* emerged as a new form of marketing theory. However, in reality, relationship marketing had been in practice for centuries.

Today, we are continuing to fine-tune marketing theory and to implement new marketing channels, but little else has changed. Although unique selling propositions have been rebranded as tipping points and database marketing has become customer analytics, the underlying principles are identical. In essence, we continue to rebrand old concepts with new names.

Indeed, marketing continues to focus on changing and reinforcing behaviors.

It is that simple. Change takes place through a relationship. By focusing on establishing, strengthening, and retaining that relationship, marketers can—and do—change behaviors by using media and marketing.

Marketing Theory Chaos

If you conduct an Internet search for marketing theories, you will find hundreds, if not thousands, of references. As you perform this search, you may also find that the term *marketing* has been diluted to mean sales or general promotion. Look at the employment ads under "marketing manager" and you will find primarily sales positions—not marketing jobs. As with many terms, the word *marketing* has become relatively meaningless without context.

When you read current marketing theory books, it becomes obvious that many focus on the esoteric, the unattainable. Most small to medium-sized businesses do not have the resources in terms of money, staff, and time to implement grand plans, which may have worked for large corporations simply because of the brute marketing force behind them and not because of their supporting theories. Marketing a local dry cleaner is substantially different from marketing an international equipment manufacturer. Therefore, many marketing theory books do not offer an actionable plan for the small to medium-sized business. That said, there have been many excellent books published about marketing theory that are very interesting to read and to discuss. Overall, however, it is most important to focus on the basics of marketing and the development of an actionable plan that fits your unique business.

Since it has many meanings, it is crucial to define marketing in actionable terms. The four Ps of marketing have been used since the 1960s to describe both the scope of marketing and the individual areas of concentration. They include price, product (or service), place (or method of distribution), and promotion (including sales, packaging, advertising, and other tools).

Each of these areas is equally important to the plan, and each area must be fully explored and implemented in order for the plan to succeed. Although some may propose other marketing frameworks or highly detailed development matrices, the four Ps is a very workable framework for planning. Through the process of manipulating and implementing the four Ps, you will be able to form your own marketing plan. We will discuss this in more detail later in this chapter.

Planning for Success

Marketing a business is a great deal like beginning a journey. You probably would not begin an important and expensive trip without a plan. At the very least, you would have a destination.

Hopefully, you also would know the mode of transportation you would use. Perhaps you would even have a written itinerary of the stops you were going to make along the way, including when your trip would be over.

If not, you might end up driving around the country without getting anywhere. Alternatively, you might rush from airport to airport, never really knowing where you were trying to go. In planning a trip, you also might include goals—such as sites to see or activities to perform. It's as simple as stating where you'd like to go, how you want to get there, what you want to do, and when you'd like to leave.

Unbelievably, many American businesses, both big and small, operate without a plan. They do not really know what they are doing or where they are going. The result is that they do not go very far or accomplish as much as they could.

By developing a sound marketing plan, however, you can control your own destiny—one of the very reasons many people are in business in the first place.

The Components of Planning

A typical outline of a marketing plan would include the following components:

- The focus, or mission, of the company
- SWOT: An analysis of strengths, weaknesses, opportunities, and threats (both for you and for your competition)
- Specific goals and strategies overall and for each product line or offering
- Specific tactics overall and for each product line or offering
- A plan to make marketing part of your company's culture
- A measurement process to gauge the success of each part of the plan
- A process for modifying the plan as necessary and repeating the process

The first mistake most people make is to begin to plan without the proper preparation. It is much like painting. Without the proper preparation, new paint will soon peel and crack. Or consider this a foundation for a house. Without the proper foundation, the house will literally fall down. Creating a marketing plan without the proper preparation produces a plan that will not last.

Most of the effort in producing a well-thought-out plan will go into preparation, not planning. However, *without the proper preparation, it is impossible to construct a successful plan.*

Following is an outline of the steps you will take to prepare to plan. Later in this book, we will examine each of the steps in detail.

Establishing Your Present Position

Before you can begin your journey, you need to assess your present situation. Often, we base our first impressions on opinions, not facts. In business, facts must always overrule opinions. Indeed, you cannot make an informed decision without information. Consider the following questions.

- What is your mission? What is the thrust of the company?
- What is your financial situation?
- What are the competitive circumstances?
- What is the acceptance factor or general image of your product or service?
- What market(s) will you target and serve?

Creating Your Mission Statement

A mission statement should briefly state why your company exists and what it intends to accomplish in the short term. Some companies also have a vision statement, which is much more forward thinking. Some companies offer a values statement as well, which puts forth the company's philosophy.

Focus your mission statement on what you wish to accomplish in the next 1 to 3 years. Your vision statement will focus on much longer-term and loftier goals. Your value statement will establish a cultural framework for your business and marketing efforts.

Everyone's mission statement will be different. A major athletic shoe company once had a very simple mission statement: **Crush X!** (They used the name of their major competitor in place of the X.)

A marketing consulting firm might have *Helping successful companies become more successful* as its mission statement. Although it may seem very simple, the statement has a great deal contained in it. First, the company will target businesses, not consumers. The businesses must be successful when the company takes them on as clients, which eliminates startups and businesses in trouble. The mission statement could go further and say, "We will provide marketing and business consulting services to successful businesses in our chosen markets and will deliver leading-edge services on time and within budget." Now more parameters have been added, such as the markets the company is interested in and the types of services it will deliver. If a prospective client asked, "Can you design and print a brochure for us?" the answer would be "No, but I can recommend someone" based on this mission statement, since the company is providing consulting services, not printing or other deliverable items.

Don't worry about creating a flowery mission statement—keep it simple. Then test all your activities to make sure you are staying true to your mission.

For example, a company has the mission statement "Helping indigenous weavers in Guatemala sustain their culture through tourism and fair trade." This contains a social statement as well as the strategies the company will employ. When someone in this company says, "Gee, shouldn't we lobby the Guatemalan government to provide social services to the indigenous weavers?" the answer would be "no," since the mission of the company focuses on tourism and fair trade—not lobbying.

You can use your mission statement to help guide you in making future business decisions. It needs to state that you will provide services within a certain area due to the cost of travel and delivery. If you have a potential client from outside your stated area, then you would probably have to say no to them because the situation would not be profitable due to the increased costs involved. As much as you would like to serve everyone, you cannot, and your mission statement can help you make determinations such as this.

The Short Mission Statement

Mission statements may be as long or short as needed to include the required information.

Overall, a short mission statement may be the best starting point, in that it will encompass the primary elements of your business without becoming mired in details. You can always expand on your mission while developing your strategies and tactics. Following are example mission statements.

1. National coffee retailer: Our mission is to inspire and nurture the human spirit—one person, one cup, and one neighborhood at a time.

2. Auto parts store: It is our mission to provide personal vehicle owners and enthusiasts with the vehicle-related products and knowledge that fulfill their wants and needs at the right price. Our friendly, knowledgeable, and professional staff will help inspire, educate, and solve problems for our customers.

3. Insurance company: To combine aggressive, strategic marketing with quality products and services at competitive prices to provide the best insurance value for consumers.

4. International milling/food enterprise: To unlock the potential of nature to improve the quality of life.

5. Software developer: We work to help people and businesses throughout the world realize their full potential. This is our mission. Everything we do reflects this mission and the values that make it possible.

6. A longer mission statement *(In this mission statement, the company chose to address some of its corporate values. Some companies separate their mission/vision/values into separate documents.)*—Airline: Workforce diversity gives us access to a world of different ideas and perspectives. We are committed to maintaining a corporate culture where men and women of all ages, races, physical abilities, preferences, and backgrounds are treated with dignity and respect. We recognize that when diversity is valued and respected, the results are improved service, customer satisfaction, and a positive community image. We believe our employees make a world of difference and work to maintain an environment where diversity and inclusion is a critical component of our success. Our Diversity Vision is to build a high-performing environment where individual differences and contributions of employees, customers, and business partners are respected and valued, the result of which is a business organization where fairness, trust, and integrity govern relationships and the way we do business.

Use the following form to create your short mission statement. Make notes and then use a separate sheet for your mission statement.

The Mission Statement of _____

- What is the primary mission or reason you are in business?
    Example: To repair computers for small businesses

    _____

    _____

    _____

- What terms or methods will you use to measure your success?
    Example: Number of customers, market penetration, gross sales

    _____

    _____

    _____

- What markets or industries will you focus on?
    Example: Northeastern Nebraska, Internet with a focus on northeastern United States

    _____

    _____

    _____

- For what qualities will your company be recognized?
    Example: Speed, cost, service, location, access
    Note: Never say "quality"—define it.

    _____

    _____

    _____

- What limits will you impose on your product or service offerings?
    Example: We will *not* . . . , We do not *want* to . . . , We *will* offer . . . (24-hour service, overnight shipping, weekend work)

    _____

    _____

    _____

- What attributes will you emphasize to achieve your goals?
  Example: Training, education, experience, staff, cost, speed

  _____

  _____

  _____

- What commitments are you willing to make in which areas?
  Example: Money, time, travel, time away from home/family

  _____

  _____

  _____

Now, using this information, write a short, concise mission statement for your company. You will have an opportunity to review and modify your mission statement later in this workbook.

SWOT

It is difficult to assess your own company's strengths, weaknesses, opportunities, and threats. After all, you are biased. You believe it will work. Although it is important for you to complete your own SWOT analysis, it will be helpful to speak with others about your SWOT as well. Ask for help from business acquaintances and vendors you respect. Asking friends and family may be interesting, but they are usually more polite than honest.

As you approach the SWOT, think of it as a matrix—with some items listed in more than one category. A strength also may be a weakness and vice versa. Or a weakness also may be an opportunity.

For example, a national floral wire service found it had excellent member florist penetration in rural areas where its competitors had weak penetration. This was an obvious strength for the company. The same positive rural penetration also showed that the company had a weakness in its lack of metropolitan market penetration. This also became an opportunity to retain the rural penetration and increase the metropolitan penetration. Moreover, the lack of metropolitan penetration became a threat.

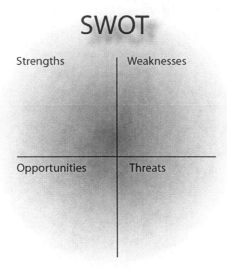

Figure 1.1. SWOT.

While this may seem confusing, creating your own SWOT matrix will aid in the development of goals, strategies, and tactics. For example, this company immediately set a goal of retaining all rural customers while increasing penetration into 10 major metropolitan areas by 20% during the ensuing 12 months.

Other examples of SWOT elements are price, location, expertise, levels of service, hours of operation, patents held, and many other elements that will be germane to your business.

Goals, Strategies, and Tactics

Setting Goals

After you have created a mission, you need to set goals—concrete goals against which you can measure your progress. You may elect to set yearly financial goals and goals regarding acquisition of market share. You also may choose to combine these concrete goals with more subjective goals, such as becoming a leader and being recognized as providing high-quality services.

For example, an established bank might have a goal of "Being known as the financial leader in its chosen markets." Although that is an excellent goal for a well-established bank, your goals may be less aggressive.

You may have goals that would include quantitative elements, such as "Obtaining X customers by X date" or "Opening two locations with $X in sales by X date."

"Surviving for a year" is not a goal. Having goals like that will quickly lead to failure. You must set your sights on a specific goal and then put *all* your efforts and resources into achieving that goal without becoming distracted.

Later in this workbook, we will look at the types of goals and how they interact with other elements.

Creating Strategies

After establishing goals, you will create strategies to achieve those goals. Strategies are the "how" of achieving your goals. For example, if your goal is to acquire 300 new customers in the next 3 months, you will need to consider how to manipulate or position your company, products, and services to achieve that goal.

Usually, strategies involve manipulating the four Ps of marketing, with only a minor focus on any "tactical" elements, which will be addressed later.

- Price
- Product
- Place (or method of distribution)
- Promotion

Each of these four elements is equal. You cannot succeed without all four. Low pricing cannot offset poor promotion. Great distribution cannot sell poorly promoted products. Moreover, nothing will destroy a bad product faster than good promotion.

Let us look at these four elements in more detail.

Price   Product
                         (or service)

TARGET

Place   Promotion
(method of delivery)

Figure 1.2. The marketing mix.

Price

Many businesses segment their markets using price. Will you be the price leader, stressing quality over cost? Or will you be the discounter, selling at low margins with a great deal of volume?

You cannot appeal to all markets, even if you have multiple product or service lines. Before you can put your final strategies in place, you have to determine what your pricing position will be.

Think for a moment about a goal of acquiring 300 new customers in 3 months in terms of pricing. How can you create a pricing structure that will help achieve that goal?

If you are a discounter, using price as a sales leader may be a path for you. You could declare yourself the discounter who will not be undersold. This type of pricing, however, requires high-frequency promotion, which will affect your tactical selections and will require a great deal of resources.

If you are in the consulting business or an extremely high-value, high-price business, your goal may be to attract three new customers in the next 3 months, as 3 new customers would double the size of your business. You may not wish to be a price leader, but to instead create value pricing, which is a fair, competitive value for your products or services, but is not a discount or a deal of any kind. Or you might position yourself as the higher-priced alternative, offering exceptional service or other benefits.

No matter which path you choose, remember it is typically easier to lower prices than it is to raise them.

An experienced retailer once said, "Never lower your price without a *reason*." Perhaps the product is the last one in your inventory and you do not plan to rebuy that item. Or perhaps the product has been discontinued. Or perhaps you have a service business and wish to use a simple service as a loss leader. Heating and air conditioning contractors will offer a "summer inspection" service at a discount that will cover the cost of their service call. At the point of inspection, the service technician may discover other services to be performed.

If you do not have a good reason to discount or lower your prices, then do not do it. Otherwise, you will simply train your customers to reward themselves with your discounts, and you will not achieve any additional marketing goals such as customer retention, buyback, or acquisition.

Product

Everyone wants to make a superior product. That is a fine attitude to have. However, it is really better to create a product or service that conforms to specific requirements. For example, coffee filters are designed for a one-time use. They are not made of the highest-quality, most durable, most expensive fibers. They must meet certain requirements, however, such as being clean and not tearing during the brewing process.

A piece of equipment, by contrast, may be sold on the merit of its durability. If yours lasts 3 years longer than your competitor's model, it is deemed a better investment.

One must examine the competitive environment as well as the sales environment in terms of what people are buying. If your market is prone to buying lower-quality items at a lower cost, you may not be able to compete against this trend with higher-priced products, even though they are of a higher quality.

Conversely, you may find that you have the most affordable item in the marketplace, even though it may not offer all the features of higher-priced competitive items.

Remember that quality should be defined as "conformance to requirements" and that the requirements are your customer's requirements, *not yours!*

Place

How you distribute your product has a big effect on your marketing plan. Will you have your own brick-and-mortar or single-purpose distribution points, such as retail stores or restaurants? Or will you manufacture or distribute goods or services for consumption through a distant distribution point, such as a baker supplying grocery stores. Alternatively, are your products to be sold via the Internet for shipment, local pickup, or both? Your methods and means of distribution are very important to your plan.

Selecting your method of distribution is extremely important. If you think you can post a website and the world will flock to your virtual door, you are probably in for a shock—in that it simply will not happen. Indeed, many items cannot be sold effectively via the Internet. A textile company learned that customers wanted to touch the cloth and see how it draped across their arms before buying. Without fulfilling their tactile sense, they were not willing to buy. In this case, the Internet served as a *reference point* but not as a *sales device*. Therefore, this textile company had to use other methods, such as stores, trade shows, direct mail sampling, and in-home sales, to promote and sell the product.

Promotion

How you tell people about your company is equally important. In fact, it is the one area where you may have the most choices. No business has infinite capital reserves to invest in promotion, so you will need to examine all the alternatives available to you before you begin to invest in promotion.

We will discuss various media later in this workbook. Overall, however, the secret to promotion is to analyze your product or service, your place, and your customer. Then determine the best way to reach that customer in a way that will appropriately highlight your product or service.

For example, say you have a machine shop, serving light industry. Using television, radio, newspaper, or other consumer media would probably reach your target customers. However, you also would be paying to reach many people who are not your target customer. This waste would consume your resources very quickly and would not achieve the desired results.

Instead, you should identify your prospects and use a combination of direct sales, direct mail, and direct promotion through newsletters or other informational campaigns. Notice the directness of this type of promotion. In this case, it is best to use a rifle, not a shotgun.

If your machine shop is a very large national enterprise catering to a distinct audience, such as custom motorcycle enthusiasts, then you could use a "shotgun" approach in national trade magazines targeting motorcycle enthusiasts. But this is not general consumer media—it is national or regional media focused on a single group of potential consumers.

Discounting

Whether price discounting should be discussed as part of pricing or promotion is a moot point—as long as it is discussed.

Discounting is an addictive and dangerous process. One might argue that if you must discount your product in order to sell it, your pricing is too high. Others argue that pricing should be increased so that it can then be discounted from time to time so as to look like a deal to encourage an immediate purchase.

Discounting and couponing have changed over the years. By the late 1960s, couponing was a common practice. Its goal was to stimulate product trial resulting in new customer acquisition. Offer a prospective customer a 25-cent discount on soap; the customer tries the brand and then becomes a repeat customer. It was a simple and effective marketing scheme.

A discounting promotion was originally intended to be a temporary tool to gain interest in a product or service. The theory was that a price promotion would increase sales or usage to a new level. Once the promotion ended, the increases would be sustained through proper customer service and sales efforts.

However, like any addictive drug, retailers thought that if a little bit of promotion was good, a lot of promotion had to be better. Ignoring the theory of promotion as a temporary lift tool, promotion became a full-time marketing tool. Even worse, it became addictive to consumers, who came to expect a deal or discount.

Today, most international couponers agree that they are rewarding existing customers with discount coupons and that the goal of couponing has shifted from customer acquisition to customer retention—especially among parity products with little brand loyalty.

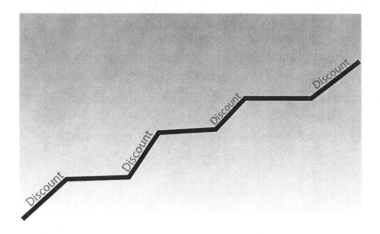

Figure 1.3. Discount promotion as a lift tool.

Unfortunately, some industries are overwhelmed by discounting. Beware. Do not follow this path: A major soft drink manufacturer explained that at least 80% of its sales are based on a deal or discount of some kind. This industry is one of many to use price as its only major wholesale marketing thrust. It simply cannot sell at full price because it has trained the wholesale buyer to expect a discount. Retailers, however, either have absorbed those discounts (kept them for themselves) or pass on only a fraction of the savings to the consumer—effectively rendering the sell-through to the consumer useless.

In direct consumer sales, entire industries—such as the pizza business—became addicted to discounting, and there does not appear to be a way for them to recover. Today, the majority of pizza sales are based on an available coupon or a price promotion that not only destroys profitability but also trains the customer to wait until the next coupon is available before they buy. Pizza is one of the few consumer food products that costs less now than it did in 1980.

After fighting the discounting model for several decades and conducting many "discount rehab" camps for manufacturers and wholesalers, it became obvious to the author that the trend was far too well entrenched to overcome. Today, some must embrace the discount model, as it would be too costly to overcome. Yet, for others, it may not be too late to avoid this pitfall.

If you are fortunate enough to be in an industry or business that is not already addicted to discounting, consider how you might use discounting on a seasonal basis or as a loss leader—then measure the results before you repeat the process.

Or use someone else's product or service as the sales enticement. Instead of discounting your product, provide a giveaway item from another company. For example, work with a local theater to give away movie tickets with the purchase of a meal from your restaurant. The theater receives free promotion as part of your advertising campaign and you get a free premium to use in your promotion. Neither product is cheapened in terms of image, and everyone—including the consumer—wins.

There are excellent uses for discounting. However, use them sparingly and remember discounting is a dangerous, addictive practice. Beware!

Tactics

Tactics are the "tools" used during the implementation of the plan. Every tactic should be considered in terms of how well it fits established goals and strategies. For example, if the target audience is composed of females who live in a specific zip code, have an annual income of $60,000, and are between the ages 24 and 54, you can conduct media research to determine which medium or tactic will best reach this target audience.

Tactics include

- newspaper;
- radio;
- television;
- websites;
- Internet advertising;
- signage;
- sales;
- telemarketing;
- direct mail;
- e-mail campaigns;

- billboards;
- transit posters;
- banners;
- brochures and other printed pieces;
- videos, DVDs, and CDs;
- specialty advertising (giveaways);
- flyers;
- sky writing;
- plus any other tools used to achieve the goals and strategies.

As noted in the following section, tactics must be considered only after goals and strategies have been determined. A plan should never begin with tactics.

Specific Goals, Strategies, and Tactics

Once you have established your position and mission by studying each element and answering the questions, you will need to define your goals in various areas. Following are a few examples of areas you will need to consider.

Setting Financial and Cultural Goals

Every business must be profitable, so making a profit is not a goal—*it's an expectation*. When you consider your *financial goals*, think in terms of whether this will be a full-time business that will support your family or a part-time venture that will simply bring in extra cash. Establishing your financial objectives with the appropriate underlying financial information will set the stage for the rest of your plan.

When it comes to *cultural goals*, you should think in terms of how many hours per week you are willing to work and how this company will influence your personal and family life. In addition, you should think about *your own values* and apply them to the plan. For example, one can make a great deal of money selling illegal drugs. However, your ethics or fear of prison may keep you from pursuing that goal. Or perhaps you're a consultant who works with large corporations, but you choose not to work with tobacco companies. These elements are parts of the vision statement mentioned previously.

Creating Strategies to Achieve These Goals

When you begin your strategic planning, forget about the details for a moment and concentrate on your broad objectives. This is strategy—not implementation. The overall strategies you will use to achieve your goals are similar to a road map. It is often as important to decide which strategies *not* to employ as it is to decide which you will employ. For example, a strategy could be to focus on the manufacture of nuts, but not bolts, for sale to aftermarket retailers in the plumbing industry.

Beware the majority fallacy. You cannot successfully be all things to all people. Pick a niche and stay there! For example, a company may employ a "third-party vendor" strategy, whereby it is a background vendor to another company and does not interact with the end customer. This strategy says the company will market only to companies allied to their field but not to the end user. Conversely, a company's strategy could be to construct large buildings coast to coast and to become a major retail entity.

A significant part of your strategy will involve your target audience. For example, if your product is sold to purchasing agents and engineers, then there is no reason to target consumers or to use consumer media, as it would just be a waste of money. Instead, you would utilize industry publications and direct marketing. (Target marketing is addressed in greater detail later in this workbook.)

And no matter what, *make sure your strategies match your goals and your mission.* Otherwise, you will dilute your efforts—and dilute your profits as well.

Determining Tactics

Typically, many people want to start their marketing plan at a tactical level. This is a classic—and extremely dangerous—mistake. Those who choose to use, for example, direct sales or radio ads without first completing their goals and strategies will most likely see their business fail.

On the contrary, once the goals and strategies are set, the tactics will write themselves, so to speak—the appropriate media or processes will become evident. For example, one part of your strategic development will be to select a target audience. The instant you select an audience, the media you will employ will come into focus. If you are targeting adults aged 18 through 34, newspaper advertising will not be as effective as other media, since this group is well known for not reading newspapers. This is the sort of information you will gain during your research phase.

Goals, Strategies, Tactics Examples

A marketing plan also can have multiple goals—each with its own strategies and tactics. Following is an example of one part of a marketing plan for a quick-serve restaurant.

- **Goal**: Increase sales on Tuesday nights
- **Strategy**: Target females 18–34 (Research shows they are the decision makers in the household, and these women are in their child-bearing years, which means many of them have a family to feed.)

    Offer a "free salad bar" for Mom with the purchase of a medium meal and free game tokens for the kids.
- **Tactic**: Radio

    Use evening drive-time slots on radio stations with affluent female listeners aged 18–34 in your restaurant's zip code (based on media and food consumption research).

Goals, strategies, and tactics also apply to a service business, as this example shows for a medical home service provider:

- **Goal**: Gain market share (new customers) in south Tulsa
- **Strategy**: Hire service providers from competitors already serving this area and offer bonuses for client conversion.
- **Alternate strategy**: Promote services via pharmacists in the targeted area and promote services directly to service recipients with a "free first visit" offer and a "free paperwork filing" offer.
- **Tactic**: Direct telephone solicitation
- **Alternate tactic**: Direct mail to targeted consumer lists based on age/income and direct mail/personal visits to pharmacists.

Now take a few moments to jot down your goals, strategies, and tactics in the spaces provided. You may wish to have several sets of each—one set for the company as a whole and one set for each product or service offering.

- **Goal (what you wish to achieve):**

  _____

  _____

  _____

- **Strategy (how you are going to achieve it):**

  _____

  _____

  _____

- **Tactics (the tools you will use):**

  _____

  _____

  _____

Assessing Your Capabilities

"Can we really do this?" It is easy to answer this question with a resounding "yes!" However, the rate at which businesses fail indicates success is not easy. In order to determine if you can really achieve your goals, examine the following:

- Your capacity: How much can you truly deliver? If you are in the service industry, how many calls can you really make? How many hours per week can you perform services? As a manufacturer, how many items can you produce and in what time frame? For example, one startup company approached the QVC channel with a product. QVC welcomed the product but needed 15,000 units, which was too large a production run for the company.
- Your requirements: What will you need in the way of staff, money, equipment, and facilities? Compare your requirements

to your resources. Can you afford your requirements? Can you effectively manage them?

- Your present situation: What is your present position in the marketplace? Do you have a realistic chance to succeed? Can you *prove* there is enough of a need for your product or service to warrant your projected success?

In addition, you must consider willingness. Many of us are *capable* of undertaking certain challenges, but we are not willing to do so. For example, most of us are capable of walking across a balance beam that is 10 feet long, 6 inches wide, and 3 feet above the ground. However, if that same balance beam is 1,000 feet in the air, not many of us are willing to walk across it. The same applies to some of the tasks of business. Of the strategies you have chosen, which are you *willing* to undertake in order to succeed?

Developing Short-Term and Long-Term Plans

You will also need to develop a plan for staffing, inventory, distribution, and all the functional components of your business to make sure they are in agreement with your marketing thrust.

Before you begin to map out your strategic plan, however, it is necessary to make some *assumptions* and obtain or confirm some basic background information.

Basic Assumptions

In order to begin the planning process, you will have to make some assumptions about your business:

- Are you an innovator or an imitator? Innovators create new products or services to meet a new need. Imitators refine or improve existing ideas that have proven successful.
- What are your geographic limits for distribution? You must set boundaries for your operation. Many times, your financial limitations will dictate these imaginary boundaries. Make sure you can adequately serve the areas you have selected. One of the worst things you can do is to be overly aggressive and then

disappoint customers with poor performance. Also consider
the cost of gasoline or other travel expenses, which may make
it unprofitable for you to deliver your service to specific areas,
even though you can sell there.

- Do you wish to have a small or a large staff? Not everyone is
willing or capable of managing a large company. Be sure you
know in your own mind what you are capable of doing and
what you are willing to do.

- Is your company held privately or by stockholders? Both
forms of ownership have positive and negative attributes. The
method you select dictates much of how your business is run
and, thus, how you will market it.

If you are a business owner, most of these factors are within your control. You will be the one to select the answer. However, other factors are
not within your control, including the following:

- *The economy.* A sudden shift in the economy will have an effect
on your business. Explore your options so you can be ready to
react to either a quick upturn or a quick downturn.
- *Societal changes.* How strong will demand be for your product
or service in 10 years? As a society changes, so do its purchasing habits. Be aware of upcoming shifts and explore how they
will affect your business.
- *Demographic shifts.* Today, America is aging. In a few years,
it will become much younger. Sound incongruous? It's
demographics, pure and simple. Demographers can predict
population changes over the next 25 years with incredible
accuracy. Use this information to project how large or small
your target audience will be in the coming years.
- *Government regulation.* Businesses, especially small businesses,
are affected by regulation. Make sure you are aware of all pending legislation that could affect your operation.
- *Competition.* It is a primary rule of business. Know your
competition.
- *Changes in technology.* The electronic calculator replaced the
adding machine. The makers of carbon paper lost most of their

corporate market share to photocopier manufacturers. Often, your largest competitor may be a single technological advance. Be aware of upcoming changes and you will be able to react to them positively.

* *Other factors beyond your control.* You cannot control a snowstorm, a hurricane, or other acts of nature. You cannot control a local plant closing that will lay off 1,000 workers. However, you can—and should—be aware of the factors that are beyond your control, and you can react to them. You can have an "eye of the hurricane" sale or offer discounts to unemployed workers, for example.

Even though you cannot control these factors, you will have to make certain assumptions about each category and how it will affect your business. In order to do that, you will need *facts*. Later in this manual, you will complete worksheets that will aid you in developing all the elements of your plan. Before you can do this, you will need to gather some basic facts.

In Summary

Planning your work and working your plan are paramount to your company's success. To create your plan, you will need to do the following:

1. Define *marketing* and apply the four Ps to your plan.
2. Develop your own mission statement for the company.
3. Analyze your SWOT.
4. Establish goals, strategies, and tactics for your plan.
5. Create a matrix of the four Ps of marketing for your company.
6. Assess your capabilities and desires.
7. Be aware of the factors that are beyond your control.
8. Learn that you will create a financial marketing statement that will be a driving force in your business plan.

In this chapter, you have started to develop the basics of your plan. You will continue to modify this information as you work through this book.

CHAPTER 2

Doing Your Homework

Base Your Plan on Fact, Not Opinion

Most people think their business will be successful: *"My product is better than anyone else's"* or *"It's the only business of my kind in town—I'll have all the business I can handle."*

This is a common and unfortunate misunderstanding of marketing. It assumes a product or service will sell just because it is better or because it is the "only show in town." What if, however, your better product costs five times as much as your competitor's product? What if you are the only supplier of snowblowers in Miami, Florida? Chances are you will not fare well. Sales will be meager. Your promotions will fail. Soon, you will join the 80% of businesses that fail within the first 2 years of their existence or the 90% that fail within 10 years.

To be successful, you need to find out a few things before you start your marketing plan. You need to determine the following:

- What is your primary target market?
- What is your secondary target market?
- Who is in your target market(s)? How can you identify them?
- What is the size, shape, and location of your market?
- What products or services will you bring to each target market?
- What is the life cycle of your product/service?
- Who are your competitors?
- What are the current market trends and future market trends?
- What will it cost to acquire sales?

Define Your Target Market

One of the most important aspects of a marketing plan is to define "who, what, when, where, why, how, and how often" regarding your product or service offerings.

Depending on the product or service, industry publications and other research sources may tell you exactly who your buyer is as well as who your end user is. Although common sense is an important aspect of selecting a target market, the facts must rule. Research is the key to selecting the appropriate target. Thinking "I bet those people will buy it" is a foolhardy and expensive way to fail. Use primary and secondary research instead.

In order to understand your target market, you will need to know the following:

- Who are your prospects and customers?
- Where do they live?
- Which media do they use?
- What are their cultural habits?
- What motivates them to buy?
- How will they use your product or service?
- Where do they live or work?
- How old are they?
- How much do they earn?
- Do they have families?
- Are they the primary consumers or do they buy for others at work or in the family?

Focus on Your Prospects

Why will these prospects purchase your goods or services?

- Do consumers or businesses use your product or service?
- Are you providing something that is a necessity or an optional purchase?
- What feelings do your customers have when they purchase? Are they happy to be making the purchase or—as with most repair services—unhappy?
- Is there a large demand for your product or service? Will the demand last for a long time?
- Are other companies meeting the need your product or service meets? If not, are you sure there is a strong need for the product or service? If so, how well is the need being met? How do you intend to serve the marketplace better?
- Is your product purchased frequently? Occasionally? Once in a lifetime?

By identifying the needs and motives of your buyers, you will be able to formulate strategies to motivate them. Use the following tables as a guide to build your own customer profile for your products or services. Do not try to complete all the categories now. You need to leave room for the new information you will learn during your research stage. One of the purposes of these tables is to help you discover what you do not know. After reading through the following chapters, you can return and complete the table fully.

Table 2.1. Sample Marketing Matrix

Product	List each product or service separately. Each may be listed several times if it appeals to multiple markets.
Target market*	List each target by type, for example, consumer homemakers, food packaging equipment manufacturers, and so forth.
Buying potential*	Gauge each market's total buying potential based on consumption and competitive information.
Geography*	List specific geographic areas of concentration.
Demography*	Specify any common demographic information, such as age, income, marital status, college education, employed part time, minimum household income of $_____, and so forth.
Psychographics*	List the reasons customers want to buy. Is this purchase a necessity? A luxury? Are they purchasing for themselves or someone else? How do they feel when they purchase your product or service?
Seasonality*	Most businesses have a season or period of time during which they sell the most (and the least). Capitalize on peak selling seasons by knowing what yours is.
Strategies	What strategies will you employ to turn this prospect group into customers?
Tactics	What marketing tools will you use to achieve your goals?
Overall ranking	Rate this group as a primary or secondary market. Or rank this group using a number system of 1–10 to indicate its overall importance to your success.

*All of this information is available to you via industry sources and publications, the local library, the U.S. Census Bureau, and online sources. Be sure to confirm any information found on the Internet with at least two other sources. Or you may wish to hire a marketing firm to assist you in this area.

List each product or service separately. Each may be listed several times if it appeals to multiple markets. Now use the following pages to complete your marketing matrix. You may wish to photocopy these pages.

Product
Target market
Buying potential
Geography
Demography
Psychographics
Seasonality
Strategies
Tactics
Overall ranking

Develop Your "Benefits Package"

What are the benefits of your product or service? Not the facts and features, but the benefits to the buyer. It is easy to become so engrossed in our work that we miss the point of what makes our product or service attractive to the end consumer.

We must remember that people do not buy a product or a service—they buy the *effect* of that product or service. For instance, you may be thrilled with the fact that your lawn mower has a larger engine than the competition's has. Regardless of that feeling, the true benefit to the customer is not the size of the engine; it is that the mower will cut the lawn faster. When a consumer buys a drill and ¼-inch drill bits, he really did not want the drill—he wanted ¼-inch holes.

Make sure you look at *why* the consumer should prefer your product or service from his or her viewpoint—not yours.

Is your product or service

- Less expensive than your competitors'?
- More durable?
- Faster?
- More convenient?
- Better performing?
- Available via a more convenient channel?

Now rank the importance of each benefit. By ranking these items, you will form a "selling platform" for your business.

Service or Product A: _____

    Rank benefits in order of importance to the *end user*:

1. _____
2. _____
3. _____
4. _____

Service or Product B: _____

    Rank benefits in order of importance to the *end user*:

1. _____
2. _____
3. _____
4. _____

Service or Product C: _____

    Rank benefits in order of importance to the *end user*:

1. _____
2. _____
3. _____
4. _____

Service or Product D: _____

    Rank benefits in order of importance to the *end user*:

1. _____
2. _____
3. _____
4. _____

Service or Product E: _____

    Rank benefits in order of importance to the *end user*:

1. _____
2. _____
3. _____
4. _____

Service or Product F: _____

    Rank benefits in order of importance to the *end user*:

1. _____
2. _____
3. _____
4. _____

Segment Your Market

In any business, there are customers who are most likely to buy and customers who will purchase more often or in greater quantities. Use the information at hand to segment your markets into groups based on their usage patterns. Common rankings include heavy users, moderate users, and light users. By dividing your market into prospect groups by age, income, gender, and geography, you will be able to determine which groups hold your greatest market potential.

Determine Market Size

After you are able to describe the general characteristics of your prime customers, where to find them, and what motivates them to purchase, you need to make sales projections. However, to project sales accurately, you need to know the size of each marketplace. By using available statistics or conducting primary research, you can identify how many potential customers you have and how often they purchase your type of product or service.

This is an extremely important step. If you do not identify the size of each usage group, you could make the classic error of assuming that the target group you have identified as your heavy user is also the largest group. But what if your heavy users are the smallest group of prospects? It may be that moderate users make up your largest group. In any case, you need to confirm the market size and the sales potential so you will know whom to target.

Unfortunately, many business owners do not relish the thought of digging through piles of statistics. It is not an easy job, but you must do it in order to succeed. By analyzing the marketplace and its potential, you can accomplish the following:

- Set specific goals and objectives based on facts, not dreams. You will know your sales potential, instead of assuming it. You will be able to measure your progress in a meaningful way.
- Gain funding, if desired. Investors want to see quantified, verified, factual information. You cannot develop a proposal with a balance sheet without facts. This is where your numbers will come from.
- Identify market trends. You want to participate in a growing marketplace, not one that is declining.
- Identify the *strengths, weaknesses, opportunities,* and *threats* (SWOT) present in the general marketplace as well as in your own company and in your competitors' companies.

Gather Your Information

Many industries publish the information you need in trade journals, directories, and other periodicals. Trade associations publish a wealth of information as well. The Internet also is an excellent resource, but be sure to watch out for noncredible sources. Before you begin, make a list of the information you need. For example, you will need to know the following:

- Size of the industry
- Comparative growth information for the past 10 years (to find out if the market has been growing or shrinking)
- Geography of the marketplace
- Usefulness of the marketplace (to find out if it is expanding)
- Market capacity versus end-user need

Then call your local library, chamber of commerce, university, election board, and city hall of records. They can quickly tell you if the information you require is readily available. If not, you may have to conduct your own research. There are three general areas to explore:

1. *Geography.* Map out your territory. Identify where your customers are. Identify your ability to reach them with your promotional messages and delivery network. Regardless of what you find, do not make the mistake of assuming your product or service is national.

Just because the majority of Americans use washing machines does not mean you can operate a national washing machine repair service from your hometown.

2. *Market size and demographics.* Identify the number of buyers in the area and their profit potential. For example, if you are selling to consumers, you can base income information on tax rolls. You can associate the number of school enrollments with the approximate age of families. Census information can give you demographic facts. Local newspapers, radio stations, and television stations also conduct consumer research that they will share with you. Usually, the only price you will have to pay is sitting through a sales pitch. Do not, however, make any promotional or media decisions yet. Accept their information with the knowledge that their medium may not be right for you.

3. *Market potential.* Translate the number of buyers into the number of potential purchases. Trade associations and publications may be able to supply information regarding purchasing patterns. City tax auditors may be able to supply information based on annual taxes paid. Do not rely on any one source of information, though. Obtain as many different sources as possible to guard against the possibility of error. The more sources you use to gauge your market potential, the clearer your end picture will be.

By using these data to make assumptions, you will be able to quantify your marketing projections, and you will be able to identify your greatest source of potential revenue. The "80-20 rule" often holds true—20% of your customers will account for 80% of your business. Therefore, it is important to identify these customers and direct the majority of your efforts toward them.

After listing your sales potential by area, you can plot where to locate your competition. Now rank them both by current sales and by their growth patterns. If your competitors are public companies, study their annual reports. Do not immediately assume you want to challenge your largest competitor. You may want to compete with smaller companies for a special niche. You can gain much of this information by speaking with vendors and suppliers who are involved in this line of business. In a business setting, speaking with potential customers is also an excellent source of information.

Identify your markets for each of your products or services. Make sure you list both primary and secondary markets for each. Your primary market will be the one that will most readily buy your goods or services. Your secondary markets will buy less but will be worthwhile targets. Ignore all questionable targets.

Depending on your business, you may need a separate plan for each geographic market because of regional differences.

Sample Market Segmentation Matrix

The following matrix shows how to compare two similarly populated areas based on the selected sales channel and population density.

The selected channel, or sales path, in this example is door-to-door (D2D) solicitation. A major telephone company chose this method to boost closing rates. Its overall media strategy was to use major media such as television to create an image and then to use D2D sales to close. They considered the elements shown in the following table

	Geography	Demographics	Size	Potential	Cost of sales	(low/high/medium)
Service A: Primary	Wagoner County	Median income: $55,948	Pop.: 73,085 Persons/ sq. mi.: 128.8	Growth: 27.1%	.25% penetration @$100 = $18,271	High due to low pop. density and selected tactic of D2D sales
Service A: Secondary	Broken Arrow, OK	Median income: $53,507	Pop.: 88,314 Persons/ sq. mi.: 1,663.9	Growth: 9.8%	.25% penetration @$100 = $22,078	Low due to pop. density

Observations

In this example, with a higher density in a more targeted area we could gain more sales more quickly—and at a lesser cost—if we switched the primary and secondary markets. What other issue do you see? Hint: Look at the growth rates.

_____

_____

_____

Now complete the following form using your products and services.

	Geography	Demographics	Size	Potential	Cost of sales (low, high, medium)
Primary					
Secondary					

Conclusions

In Summary

1. Create a plan. This is a required component for your success. Without a written plan, it is extremely difficult to stay on track and achieve your goals.
2. Create each part of your plan based on verifiable facts—not conjecture or opinions. Research must be an integral part of your planning process. The Internet, the local library, and trade associations are often excellent sources of qualified information.
3. Define your marketplace and your target customers rather than trying to be all things to all people, often called the *majority fallacy*. You must define your customer and then target only that customer. Otherwise, your efforts will be weak and diluted.
4. Develop your matrix of product or service benefits. Just what are you going to sell? Many entrepreneurs try to sell far too many products or services and their business lacks focus. You must define each product or service and then analyze it to determine its profit potential.
5. Create your own SWOT analysis. Examining your strengths, opportunities, weaknesses, and threats can be a difficult task. Engage your professional peers in a SWOT review—or retain a professional to help. Having a clear picture of your SWOT will help you build the right plan for your company.

CHAPTER 3

Competing Effectively

You cannot avoid it. If you are operating in a business that has any sales potential, you have competition. Competition is one of the most basic elements of business. The best way to cope with competitive pressures is to identify your true competitors and concentrate your efforts on exploiting their weaknesses—and all businesses have weaknesses, no matter how large or small they may be.

Identifying Your Competitors

There are two general types of competitors:

1. Those who supply services or products that are identical or very similar to yours. This also may be a "commodity" business.
2. Those who have dissimilar products or services, but are competing for the same disposable income (share of wallet or budget). For instance, consumers have a finite budget for entertainment. Therefore, theaters, amusement parks, movie rental businesses, bookstores, and so forth are all competing for the same disposable income.

Once you have identified your competition, put yourself in their place. Analyze their market segmentation. Are they competing for the same market? Many times, companies offering like products or services are not competing for the same market and can peacefully coexist. If you believe you have a real competitor, find out what their niche is.

For example, Company A develops software for national and international catalog companies. Company B also develops software, but does not offer software specifically for catalogs. Even though both companies develop software, they are not true competitors.

This also is evident in women's retail clothing. High-end and discount retailers both sell women's clothing. However, they are not competitors, since they have completely different target audiences.

By contrast, most food vendors are competitors, even though they offer vastly different menus. They are all competing for "share of eating out" wallet.

When you analyze your competitors, think of them in these terms:

- Which of the following are their strengths?
  - Price
  - Innovation
  - Convenience
  - Location
  - Quality
  - Field service
  - Reputation
  - Expertise
- Is their company on the upswing or downswing?
- Has their position in the marketplace improved over the past 10 years? Why and how?

Learn all you can about their pricing, costs, and methods of distribution. Study their pricing and promotional habits. Most important, study their weaknesses. Look for ways to capture a part of the market that they do not wish to have or cannot control.

Turning Competitor Weaknesses Into Your Strengths

By completing the following chart, you will be able to match each of your products or services to a competitor and list their strengths and weaknesses. By comparing your strengths to their weaknesses, you will identify opportunities or threats.

For example, remember the floral wire service mentioned earlier? Let's take their case further. As we noted in the SWOT (strengths, weaknesses, opportunities, and threats) analysis, this company's primary competitor held the majority of the metropolitan markets and the smaller company was having a difficult time convincing florists to use their service. By comparing its strengths and weaknesses to those of its larger competitor, the company was able to find an opportunity.

To review, the larger, established company had a great dominance in major markets and urban areas. The smaller company had very poor market penetration in the metro areas, with substantial penetration into rural areas. Based on this information, the smaller company promoted itself and the larger company as "the perfect combination." The strategy held that florists needed both wire services to be effective—the larger service for metro areas and the smaller service for suburban and rural areas. This allowed the smaller service to stimulate trial of their services among a larger customer base without having to compete directly with the larger service. In short, they turned a negative into a positive.

Another example is a national baked goods company with spotty national distribution and heavy concentration in southern states. When this company decided to roll out a line of cookies, it guessed that it would be too small for the large competitors to notice. It also used a warehouse distribution channel, whereas its largest competitors used store-door delivery. Eventually, it stopped producing cookies, as its national competitors literally drove the company out of every market. Its warehouse distribution costs were high and diluted profitability (slotting allowances in Los Angeles alone were $250,000), and its warehouse distribution method hindered success. Even though one national cookie brand rates worst in taste tests, it is the best-selling cookie in the United States simply because of its distribution channels and size. Indeed, influence and distribution overcomes quality and taste every time—in the same category.

For a third example, let's look at a commodity business—commercial printing. Commercial printing is a commodity because the industry has used pricing to differentiate itself and has dug itself into a discounting hole. In addition, although printers may have different equipment or technology, end users view their products as the same. Printers, of course, want to show how their quality is better—but the differences are not self-evident to the end users. Printing also is not a sole-source service for most customers, who often distribute their printing business among several printing companies, which is a wise practice.

After decades of competing based on price, one international printer decided to survey its clients to find out how the clients chose a printer. Although the survey covered many technical and service aspects—all of

	Bruce's	Lowe's/Home Depot	Local Ace	Local one-off
Strengths	• Deeper selection (more items in same categories) • Near big-box stores • Curbside parking, no-hassle shopping	• Lower prices, broad selection • Name, image, national advertising • Hours • Credit	• Name, image, national advertising • Deep selection • Paint selection • Curbside parking, no-hassle shopping	• Well-known, longtime resident • Hard-to-find parts • Known as price leader • Curbside parking, no-hassle shopping
Weaknesses	• Narrow selection	• Broad but shallow selection • Crowded, poor parking	• Narrow selection	• Junky store • Not keeping up with the times • No paint or large power tools • Poor location in "razor wire" neighborhood • Limited hours
Opportunities (for Bruce's)	Show price leadership and product/service difference	Could collaborate with big-box store as referral for special plumbing supplies		
Threats	Big-box store can trample local store			
Notes				

which were viewed as parity items by the customers—it revealed something the printers had not considered.

"It's the shrimp," said one of the survey respondents. Many customers and accounting firms spend days and sometimes weeks working with printers at their location. These projects are often annual reports or other items that must be produced in a timely fashion. One printer fed his guests shrimp and many other foods while they were on site working. Other printers did not provide this level of customer service and hospitality. Therefore, when the client selected a printer, it was the printer's level of hospitality—not its printing capabilities—that closed the sale.

Put yourself in your customers' shoes. Ask them what they really want from you and why they buy what they buy. Armed with that information, you will be able to target their desires and close the sale.

Complete the following chart for your competition.

Performing a Competitive Analysis

The prior chart is a sample competitive analysis for Bruce's, a neighborhood hardware store. We have all shopped at hardware stores. How would you handle what the analysis reveals? Add your own comments.

Now think about your company and your competitors. Fill in the following chart and then share it with your business acquaintances and vendors you respect. See what they might add to the list.

Look at your attributes and the attributes of your competitors. What opportunities do you see? Are there any weak areas in which you need to protect yourself? Can you turn a potential negative into a positive? By analyzing this information, you will form a good informational base from which to develop your marketing strategies.

	You	Competitor #1	Competitor #2	Competitor #3
Strengths				
Weaknesses				
Opportunities				
Threats				

We will explore this in more detail, but be aware that all your marketing strategies will focus on your company's strengths and on how your company can benefit from the weaknesses of the competition.

In Summary

Everyone has competition. The key is to identify your true competitors by thinking in terms of "share of wallet" and how much share your company has. The following activities provide the framework for developing—and monitoring—competition:

1. Identifying your true competitors by defining them
2. Analyzing your competition in actionable terms
3. Turning negatives into positives
4. Monitoring your competition and revising your plan

CHAPTER 4

Identifying Marketplace Trends

Things change. There is just no way around it. Successful businesses change with the market. Those who do not embrace change often fail. By understanding change and embracing it, you can drive your company to higher levels of success.

Although it is important to look forward, it also is important to understand what has happened in your market and your geographical area during the last 15 to 20 years. Has the market changed? How have market trends affected businesses like yours? If you offer a single product or service, you must be aware of any possible technological changes—no matter how remote—that could literally put you out of business overnight.

For example, consider a manufacturer who makes cassette tapes. The advent of the DVD spelled disaster for that company in 1981. Industry experts had all agreed that cassette sales would be replaced by DVD sales. Did the company's mission allow it to shift technologies to the DVD or was it stuck with an outdated product line and no resources to make the change? Or—even worse—did the company refuse to change? By paying attention to your industry and the predictions of the experts in the industry, you can predict your own future.

Think about the funeral business. Over the past 25 years, the funeral business has boomed due to simple demographics. However, after the baby boomers are gone, the number of deaths in the United States will plummet. Fewer deaths mean fewer funerals. In addition, social mores are changing, and cremation is becoming much more popular than traditional burials. Plus, on a competitive note, major club stores now sell coffins at a huge discount. Today's funeral directors must take notice of these trends and act quickly to create a new future for their industry.

There also are trends and fads in any industry. A trend is a movement of customers in an industry. It is supported by statistics and is usually an extension of a long-term movement. This could be a brand extension, changes in packaging, changes in a delivery system, or many other forms of customer shifts. A fad, on the other hand, is short term and does not last. Pet rocks, hair hats, scratch-and-sniff T-shirts, and many other products are fads. They come, they go. As a marketer, you must embrace the fact that some of the most popular items are temporary.

Although fads and trends typically apply to products, they also impact delivery channels, marketing, and other aspects of your business. Many items that used to be delivered via U.S. mail on a CD are now downloadable via the Internet. The Internet is certainly not a fad—it is a tactically driven trend that has been growing since the early 1950s. Downloading music via the Internet may appear to be a trend, but it is really just a fad that will be replaced by direct download to cell phones or new media and methods. Flash mobs, some social media, and many other forms of promotion also are fads. Although social media in general will be with us for many more years, new media will replace many of the aspects of social media, such as texting.

Overall, remember that nothing is forever. One must study industry trends and social trends and determine what may or may not have a long life.

Use the following to identify trend areas in your industry. Remember that you can make the highest-quality, best-priced buggy whip in the world and you still cannot sell them in any great quantity.

Technological Changes

Have there been any advancements or rapid shifts in equipment or techniques in your industry?

_____

_____

_____

Demographic Changes

America is growing older. How will this affect your product or service? How large a demographic will your primary target be in 5 years? In 15 years?

Social Changes

Are you capitalizing on a craze, like the silly-shaped rubber bands, or are you building on a firmer platform, such as the acceptance of the personal computer as a work tool?

Economic Shifts

How will the current economic situation affect you? Will a dramatic change—either positive or negative—have an effect on your business?

Government Regulations

Is there any pending legislation or discussion of new regulations or taxation that will affect you if enacted?

Competitive Moves

Is the competition growing or shrinking? Are their companies on the upswing or downswing? What are the historical trends and cycles your competition has experienced?

We Are Almost Ready . . .

Now that you've identified your market, know all your strong points, can identify your best customer groups, and have fully researched your competition, you're ready to start your plan.

In Summary

You may not have a crystal ball, but you can identify trends that may affect your business, including the following:

1. Technological changes
2. Demographic changes
3. Social changes
4. Economic shifts
5. Government regulation
6. Competitive moves

By staying abreast of changes in each of these areas, you can manipulate your plan to either counter the change or capitalize on it.

CHAPTER 5

The Marketing Plan

Now that you know all that there is to know about your market, it is time to develop a plan.

Developing the Mission Statement

First, as previously discussed, you will need to develop a mission statement. What do you really want to be when you grow up? Earlier in this workbook, you completed your mission statement. However, it is now time to revisit your work in that area and refine your mission statement, your vision, and your values. Based on what you have learned so far, review and alter your mission statement focusing on the following points.

- Why are you in business?
- What do you want your company to be?
- What is the corporate mission?
- Are you going to be an innovator or an imitator?
- Will you dominate a marketplace, like General Foods, or specialize in a niche area, like Morton Salt? Or, will you operate as a reseller of someone else's goods and services?
- What is your long-term vision, including an exit plan?
- What are your values?
- Do your values match the industry in which you are operating? For example, an independent oil company expanded its business into the convenience store market. The company invested a vast amount of time and money building, opening, and operating multiple convenience stores. The personal values and beliefs of the owners were such that they refused to sell beer and cigarettes in the stores. This went against the research findings that the profits of convenience stores are derived from the sale of beer

and cigarettes and that the three top-selling items in convenience stores are beer, cigarettes, and gasoline. It did not take long for sales to lag and for profits to decline. In essence, you can do whatever you wish in your business, *but if you wish to succeed, you need to meet the expectations of your customers.*

No matter what you choose, you must have a corporate identification and mission. Simply wanting to make a profit is not enough. Profit is an expected by-product of a business, not a goal. When developing a mission, however, you must keep a *broad* purpose in mind.

For example, if a company operating in the 1890s had a corporate mission of manufacturing hardware and related aftermarket equipment for horse-drawn carriages, the advent of the automobile would have put them out of business because their mission was too narrow. Although there are still niche markets for horse-drawn carriages and wagons, they are extremely small. To be successful, this company should have had the mission of manufacturing high-quality aftermarket accessories for the consumer transportation industry. This would have allowed them to serve both the maturing buggy market and the emerging automotive market. Indeed, it would have positioned them for many technological changes as the consumer transportation market evolved.

Now take time to carefully review your initial mission statement and then refine it.

The mission statement of: _____
  What is the primary reason you are in business?

    _____
    _____
    _____

  What terms or methods will you use to measure your success?

    _____
    _____
    _____

  What markets or industries will you focus on?

    _____
    _____
    _____

For what qualities will your company be recognized?

_____

_____

_____

What limits will you impose on your product or service offerings?

_____

_____

_____

What attributes will you emphasize to achieve your goals?

_____

_____

_____

What commitments are you willing to make?

_____

_____

_____

Making Strategic Choices

Keeping the four Ps in mind (price, product, place, and promotion), you can select strategic alternatives. For example, if you wish to increase sales volume, you can enter new markets, convert noncustomers in existing markets, further penetrate segments in which you're already active, expand geographically, and expand into new demographic or socioeconomic groups. In addition, refer to your list of product benefits and your competitive analysis. You may find that you can capitalize upon a competitor's weakness. Another strategy is to increase the rate at which customers use your services by offering incentives, finding new uses for your services, or increasing the obsolescence rate of your product.

Using the information you gained early on during your research phase, you can select your customer targets based on size, growth rate, anticipated profitability, and competition. You must also select the companies with whom you wish to compete, avoiding those that are obviously too strong.

And finally, you must determine **why** the customer should buy from *you* and not your competitor. What benefits do you offer? What differential advantage do you have? This will formulate the central strategy for your marketing campaign.

One way to determine why customers buy is to ask them. "We certainly like this sprayer because of its broad coverage—why did *you* buy this one?" Customer surveys and general observation of customers will also generate information as to why people buy.

In the end, always defer to the customer's reasons, *not yours.*

Implementing Your Strategies

To continue our story of the pizza restaurant, if your goal is to become the number one family pizza restaurant in the market area, with annual sales of $2 million and a market share of 20%, your primary strategy could be to target the main decision maker of the household, whom you have identified as the female.

Through your research, you have also chosen as your competition the neighborhood pizza restaurant that may be part of a small franchise. You have also made the conscious decision not to compete with the national franchises because you cannot afford to match their marketing expenditures. Instead, you will concentrate on your differential advantage of "an old Italian atmosphere," with no games or gimmicks, offering wholesome, inexpensive pizza and related Italian food for the entire family.

In order to achieve your goal, you might use these tactics: You'll use radio advertising in predinner time slots and distribute flyers to day care centers (for Mom to take home) to advertise your low-cost, high-nutrition meals, served in a family atmosphere. You will distribute flyers in adjacent neighborhoods, send press releases to neighborhood papers, and offer to "cross-coupon" with other businesses in your area. As a tie-breaker, or added incentive for Mom to select your restaurant, you will offer her the choice of a free silk rose (obtained free from a florist also involved in the promotion) or a free trip to the salad bar on Tuesday night, which is your slowest sales night. In addition, you will train your employees in the art of suggestive selling with the goal of upgrading each sale 20% by suggesting appetizers and desserts.

Then you'll track your sales daily, recording both controllable and uncontrollable influences (weather, competitive offers, new competition, major unrelated events in town, etc.) to determine the effectiveness of your campaign.

Of course, in most marketing plans, you will have more than one market to penetrate. **Thus you will have to formulate goals, strategies, and tactics for each of your target markets and each of your products or services.**

Please note: Resist the urge to discount your products or services as a primary tactic. Discounting is addictive! Used sparingly, it can boost short-term sales and improve long-term growth by introducing your product or service to new customers, thus creating the proper buying habit. If your business is caught in a competitive environment that demands discounting, make sure you do not make the fatal error of "giving away" your product. Many times, businesses sell their products or services without making any profit in order to gain a new customer. Although this might be effective in extreme cases, it is usually detrimental in the long term.

Do not be like the owner who said, "I'm losing money on each item, but I will make up for it in volume." This truly occurs in businesses—at least until they fail.

Overused, discounting only rewards current customers and causes them to wait for the next special before they buy. Continual discounting is a downward spiral through which you will not be able to sell your goods at full market value. It can take years to repair the damage of over-zealous discounting. For a good example, just look at the retail apparel industry. When was the last time you bought clothing at full price? Most consumers wait for the next sale and then reward themselves using your discounts. Research performed by major food manufacturers also indicates that couponing typically rewards current customers and does not attract new buyers.

In Summary

1. You developed a version of your mission statement earlier in this workbook, but it is time to refine it based on your subsequent activities. In fact, it is important to review your mission—and your total plan—every 6 months. You may not make any changes, but the review is important to help you stay on track.

2. We also reviewed your vision and values to add the cultural side of your business. After all, a business must reflect your personal values as well as your business values.

3. The process of making strategic choices was illustrated. In your business, you will often be required to make strategic choices.

CHAPTER 6

Common Ways to Send a Message to Your Market

Now that you have developed your mission statement and have considered how the four Ps will influence your plan, you need to establish goals, strategies, and tactics. Before you do, you need to be aware of the tools available to you, how they work, and their relative costs. Even a master chef cannot successfully plan a meal without first knowing which types of meat and produce are readily available. By combining this information with the market research you gathered earlier, you can identify the best way to communicate with your target audience(s) in the most cost-effective manner.

As you begin to review or employ any promotional tool, make sure you measure each tool in terms of cost per person, cost per thousand, or other appropriate metric. Then measure the effects of each medium. What is the cost per sale for newspaper versus radio, for example? Based on those results, change your tactics accordingly, abandoning tools that are high cost and low impact and buying tools that have a lower cost and higher impact.

Sales Promotion Materials

Having information readily available to respond to inquiries about your company is very important. Even an inexpensively produced brochure or handout about your company can aid you in the selling process. If you plan to print materials, you will need to discuss production costs with a graphic artist and a printer before you develop your working budget. You will also need to establish a plan that predicts how many printed items you will need and what your annual usage may be.

No matter what your business, you will need to print business cards, letterhead, envelopes, mailing labels, and a host of other materials bearing your company name and logo.

These materials are the image of your company. Take special care that they are positive ambassadors for you and do not project a shoddy image.

Consumer Advertising

The theory of consumer advertising is simple: Use the media that will most cost-effectively reach your target audience. Professional media buyers do not buy types of programs in terms of content or personalities. They buy numbers. After all, it does not really matter if the radio station plays country or jazz. What matters is who is listening.

If you do not know exactly who your target prospect is, *do not advertise.* No matter how much you spend or how "good" the individual medium is, you cannot succeed unless you are talking to the right target audience. For example, preteens do not make many decisions regarding family car purchases. Therefore, if the number one radio station caters to preteens, it will not do your car dealership much good. Conversely, if you own the local dance studio, the station might be a good choice for you.

The most successful advertisers use a mix of media. They may choose a combination of print, broadcast, and outdoor media to reach their goals. However, you must select the media you use based on their individual abilities to bring strength to the mix and, thus, most effectively sell your product or service. There is no such thing as a bad medium—only one that has been misused. When reviewing the following information about media selection, also keep in mind the appropriateness of the medium for your product or service (can you explain your company on a billboard?) and the cost of producing materials to use with the medium (television spots can cost a great deal more to produce than radio). As with any set of guidelines or rules, there will be exceptions. The following information will not make you an instant expert, but will acquaint you with the available media choices.

Television

Television is an extremely powerful combination of sight and sound. You can use it to generate feelings, to create images, and to incite action on the part of the viewer.

At first glance, two elements appear certain about television—first, that it is extremely expensive, and second, that it can be used only for consumer or retail goods and services. However, although television usually requires a substantial budget (you cannot buy only one spot and expect to see results), it is often the least expensive medium because it reaches such a broad base of consumers. And you can use television to sell business services to businesses simply by selecting the proper programming and the proper target audience. Selling photocopiers during Saturday morning cartoons is not a wise use of money. However, the same ads run during a news program or special broadcast appealing to business people would be appropriate.

The art of buying television is as easy as following a few simple rules. Discard any personal likes or dislikes you may have about particular programs. Also, forget any notions you may have about types of programs, such as newscasts, soap operas, and situation comedies. And if you cannot deal with an ad agency and you choose to buy your own media, deal with television stations on the following basis:

1. Tell them specifically what your target audience is, for example, "Female homemakers 25 to 44 years old with annual household incomes of $25,000 to $45,000 who live in the central metro area."
2. Develop a schedule stressing either "reach" or "frequency." For example, if you wanted to mount an ongoing image campaign, reaching as many people as possible might be important to you. If, however, you were advertising a weekend sale, you would want to concentrate your efforts on a smaller group, but reach everyone in that group more frequently.
3. Be honest with them. Tell them exactly what you are prepared to spend. In addition, ask them to include information about gross rating points (GRPs) in their proposal. GRPs measure the relative impact of television programming. Each GRP is a number that is equivalent to 1% of the total population. Thus by buying 100 GRPs

in New York and 100 GRPs in Chicago, both schedules will have the same relative impact, even though the cost will be different. Be aware, however, that buying 100 GRPs won't guarantee that everyone will see your commercial. This is where the concepts of reach and frequency come in. Your 100 GRPs during a week might reach 20% of the population 5 times each or they might reach 10% of the population 10 times each.

4. As a rule, media buyers will also specify how many target rating points (TRPs) they wish to achieve. This is the number of GRPs the schedule will generate among your chosen target audience. Thus the schedule should show the total of both "household" rating points (GRPs) and "target" rating points (TRPs) and the average cost for each.

At this time, you should note that the price of television programming fluctuates with supply and demand as well as the total number of people who are watching. Thus a show that reaches 10,000 households should cost less than one reaching 250,000 households. In addition, the station's "inventory" will affect pricing. Each day, a television station has 24 hours to fill with programming and advertising. If they do not sell one of their commercial slots, they will lose the revenue for that time. Therefore, television time will cost more during the fourth quarter of the year, when all the retailers are clamoring to sell their Christmas wares, than during the first quarter, when many advertisers are inactive. Given the choice of introducing a campaign in December or January, the commercial time would cost significantly less in January. Of course, your product or service would have to be appropriate for that season. Generally, television commercial slots are most expensive in the fourth quarter, followed by second quarter, third quarter, and first quarter.

When you receive the proposals back from all the stations, you will be able to see which programs will deliver the most impact for your dollar by comparing the relative cost per gross rating point and the cost of the target rating points. Although many advertisers use a number of television stations for any given campaign, television is not channel sensitive like radio. Television viewers channel-hop constantly. Therefore, you are much better off ignoring your subjective feelings about specific channels and programs and paying attention to which programs will deliver the most rating points for the least money.

You must exercise some common sense, of course. The best buy is at 3:00 a.m., but will that time slot produce the best results for you? If you are advertising a product such as hamburgers, 6:00 a.m. may not be a good time, simply because hamburgers are not appealing to most people at that time of day. Not only must you analyze the numbers, but you must also look at lifestyle patterns and advertise to people when they are most receptive to your message. This is where knowing your customer becomes very important.

In addition to the cost of the medium, you will also need to consider the cost of producing a television commercial prior to making a final decision. Producing a television spot can be much more expensive than, say, producing a classified newspaper ad. You must consider these costs, as well as the cost of the time, when developing a working budget.

Radio

Radio is similar to television in that it is a broadcast medium. However, the similarity ends there. Since it involves only sound and not sight, the production costs can be much lower than television. For example, filming or videotaping a boat traveling down the Amazon River would be rather expensive. So would filming a crew climbing Mount Everest. With imagination and sound effects, however, on radio you can simulate virtually any place or situation.

The total radio audience is also more segmented. In a market with 3 television stations, there may be as many as 25 radio stations—each serving a small niche in the marketplace. In order to be effective, most advertisers will buy time on more than one station, assuming there are multiple stations that appeal to your target audience.

The principles of reach and frequency in television also hold true for radio. However, the cost of radio is calculated on the investment required to reach each 1,000 listeners, known as cost per thousand, or CPM. In addition, when looking at radio stations, you must refer to each station's ratings during each "day part." During times when more people are listening, the spots cost more. In addition, radio rates are "inventory sensitive," so the much-sought-after morning drive spots in December will cost more than the 3:00 p.m. spots in January.

To buy radio effectively, you must first identify the stations that will most effectively reach your target audience. Then you must (once again) put aside your own personal feelings and tastes. You might love country music and hate rock and roll, but that doesn't mean your target audience shares your views. Base your decision on which combination of stations will deliver the message to your target audience most effectively and efficiently. You may also find that the number one station is in such demand that their inventory is slim and their rates are very high. In this situation, you may wish to only buy the number two and three stations in your target area, since you will be able to reach the same number of target prospects at a lower CPM.

Newspapers

Daily and weekly newspapers offer you the opportunity to present a total selling message, in that you have more space in which you can tell a longer story. You can present more facts to be studied. People can reread an interesting portion of an ad. Newspaper ads have a longer shelf life than television and radio ads. Broadcast ads are fleeting, lasting only a few seconds. Print ads last as long as the reader retains the paper.

Indeed, newspapers offer a number of unique benefits. However, you must study the demographics of who reads your local newspapers and compare them to your target audience to judge the potential effectiveness of a newspaper ad. For example, if your target audience is children, newspapers are probably not a good choice, since you are paying for the entire readership and not just the few child readers. A representative from the newspaper will be able to share statistical information about the age, sex, income, and geographic location of its readers—perhaps even by the topical sections of the newspaper. In addition, you should be able to learn which issues have the highest readership and even the average time each reader spends with the paper.

By comparing these facts to what you know about your target market, you will be able to determine if newspaper is a viable medium for your media mix. If so, you can compare rival newspapers by comparing their cost per thousand readers.

Billboards

Billboards are a wonderful way to generate immediate impact throughout your chosen marketplace—as long as you do not try to put too much information on them. A headline of five words or less accompanied by a name and logo is best for a billboard. Any more and the passerby does not have time to read or absorb your message.

Outdoor boards are divided into two groups—posters and bulletins. Posters are the smaller of the two and generally have large sheets of printed paper glued onto them for periods of 30 days. Posters are usually purchased in "showings," which generally equate to levels of GRPs. Thus you can translate the cost per showing into a cost per GRP or a cost per thousand, based on the appropriate traffic counts. This will allow you to make price comparisons among the various types of media you are considering.

Bulletins are larger than posters and display a painted message. Bulletins are sold on an annual or semiannual basis, and the advertiser contracts for a specific location during the entire contract time.

The beauty of outdoor advertising is that it is big and bold and makes a quick impact. It can literally point out your business, and you can blanket a city with a new slogan using this medium. Like all the other media we have discussed, it can be a powerful component of a total campaign.

Transit Media

The sides of buses, the tops of taxis, the walls of transit shelters, and the backs of bus benches all compose a slightly different form of outdoor advertising—transit media. As on billboards, a transit ad message must be short. Reading the top of a taxi going 45 miles per hour or the side of a bus on an expressway is not easy. Therefore, the message must be short and to the point. If, however, you want your message to be seen all around town, transit advertising may have a place in your media plan. Transit media costs are based on the number of people who are exposed to your ads. By translating this information into GRPs or CPM you can compare the cost of transit advertising with other media.

Magazines

Like newspapers, magazines offer you ample space to sell your products or services. In addition, because of their printing methods and slick paper stock, most magazines offer you an excellent format for the use of color photography.

The shelf life of magazines is longer as well, with most publications issuing on a monthly or quarterly basis. Magazines can also give you information about their readership, which you can then match to your target market specifications. In addition, magazines are a bit like radio stations, in that they will appeal to a much more specific audience than newspapers. This could possibly allow you to better target the right audience with your message.

Trade Advertising

Trade Publications

If you are an industrial or vertical marketing company, consider advertising in pertinent trade journals and attending trade shows. As with consumer advertising, though, make sure your efforts are targeting the right audience.

Ask to see the publication's BPA (Business Publisher's Association) statement so you can compare their readership with competing publications. Pay particular attention to the number of copies distributed "free" and how many are paid subscriptions. Although there are exceptions to this in certain industries, readership may be higher among those who pay to receive a magazine than among those who receive a free magazine.

If you are selecting among magazines that have both paid and unpaid circulation, ask to see reader research studies conducted by outside sources. Talk with current advertisers about their successes (or failures). If the publications have reader response cards, ask to see the average number of cards returned per ad and the average number of inquiries per card. By combining all this information, you will be able to form a relatively good picture of individual publications and determine which, if any, are right for your product and service.

Following is a more detailed section regarding trade, or industry, advertising.

Industry Advertising

As with any professional process, the placement of print media, especially trade- or industry-specific media, can be segmented into primary areas. In this case, the primary process areas include discovery, analysis, negotiation, and measurement of performance.

Discovery

During the discovery process, you should create a planning framework. This framework may include the following, as appropriate:

1. *Identification of target audiences and media choices.* The marketing team must identify potential target audiences and the overall media choices that reach those audiences in each class of trade. This often is achieved by reviewing past publication performance and the editorial content of selected publications and/or aligning current or future sales targets with the appropriate media targets. The media titles initially selected are scrutinized during the analysis phase.

2. *Goal setting and measurement standards.* In order to properly place and "post," or measure, the effects of advertising, it is necessary to establish the goals of the campaign in quantitative terms and to determine the methods by which the campaign will be measured.

Campaign goals may be any combination of the following:

- *Monetary*: measured by actual sales and the relative return on investment between media invested and total sales or by incremental sales increases
- *Response oriented*: measured by cost per lead, cost per sale, or cost per fulfillment
- *Image oriented*: measured by qualitative and quantitative reader research, among many other approaches
- *Penetration focused*: measured by how well a single audience segment is penetrated by chosen messages
- *Reach focused*: measured by how widely known the company becomes because of the campaign

Publication	Gross Circ	CPM	Target Circ	Target CPM	# of Ads	Gross Impressions	Total Expense	Issue Months						Targeted Months					
								Jan	Feb	Mar	Apr	May	Jun	Jul	Aug	Sep	Oct	Nov	Dec
Education										Targeted Months	Targeted Months				Targeted Months				
Pub 1	96845	63	33812	181	7	677915	42915		1/2P4C 6845	1/2P4C 6845	1/2P4C 5845				1/2P4C 5845	1/2P4C 5845	1/2P4C 5845		1/2P4C 5845
Pub 2	29690	102	12931	234	6	178140	18120	1/2P4C 3020			1/2P4C 3020	1/2P4C 3020				1/2P4C 3020	3020	1/2P4C 3020	
Pub 3	4500	360	NA	NA	3	13500	4860			1/2P4C 1620		1/2P4C 1620			1/2P4C 1620				
Pub 4	34607	71	34322	71	7	242249	17150		1/2P4C 2450	1/2P4C 2450	1/2P4C 2450	1/2P4C 2450			1/2P4C 2450	1/2P4C 2450	1/2P4C 2450		
Health Care																			
Pub 5	27930	161	11337	398	6	167580	27064	1/2P4C 4510		1/2P4C 4510	1/2P4C 4511				1/2P4C 4511	1/2P4C 4511	1/2P4C 4511		
Retail																			
None Recommended																			
Parks & Recreation																			
Pub 6	21008	145	6757	451	3	63024	9135			1/2P4C 3045			1/2P4C 3045					1/2P4C 3045	
Pub 7	50000	81	25407	160	1	50000	4070					1/2P4C							
Total Expense							$123,314.00												

Prepared by AMSI, 10/2001

Figure 6.1. Sample media budget.

- Measurement of media typically focuses on the impact of the media (see number 2). In addition, however, media must be measured and reviewed in light of its respective readership. Each audience or industry segment has its own discounting or other niche practices. These are not under the direct control of the media or advertising, but they must be examined as part of the measurement process. Overall, measurement is often composed of a combination of tools, including the following:
- Publication reader studies
- Sales force feedback
- Lead generation via response cards and other publication tools
- Lead conversion (how many leads are successfully converted to sales)
- Cost per lead
- Cost of fulfillment
- Sales cycle (audience measurement)
- Cost per sale (audience measurement)
- Sales pricing elasticity by target market (audience measurement)
- Any specific sales system data requirements

Once the discovery process is complete, analysis of the preselected media is performed.

Media Analysis

Many years ago, it was appropriate to examine the overall number of readers for any given publication to arrive at a general cost to reach each 1,000 readers. This technique was typically followed by reviewing the cost per lead generated, as well as generally indexing publication performance using these measurements.

However, although this technique continues to be a good starting point, the media planning process must take a more segmented approach. With multiple publications in every vertical industry segment, it is necessary to determine not only the gross number of readers but also who those readers are in terms of job function and potential purchasing ability. Then their respective numbers must be isolated within the total readership. The resulting CPM for "qualified targets" provides a true picture of the publications' potential worth.

For example, if a company targeted advertising agencies to sell their graphic arts products, one might assume that *Advertising Age* would be the primary vehicle. It offers one of the lowest overall CPM rates, is highly respected, and has a strong readership. However, upon closer examination of the targeted buying audience within advertising agencies and after performing a reader segment analysis of *Ad Age*, it is easy to see that it is not the proper vehicle in that it is read by ad agency management, but not by the purchasers of graphic art supplies.

Figure 6.1 shows how gross CPM and qualified target CPM differ, bringing another component to the decision-making process.

Negotiation

All trade media are negotiable. Areas of negotiation typically focus on rate reduction and merchandising assistance.

Rate Reduction

Rate reduction is part of the traditional dickering over media prices. The extent to which a publication will discount its rates is often dependent on current market conditions as well as industry conditions. In addition to simple rate discounting, rate holder ads can be used to achieve a better rate within a publication's frequency grid. By placing, for example, 6 large ads and 6 small ads, an overall 12-time rate is established, reducing the total expense while promoting the advertiser year-round.

Merchandising

All merchandising is dependent upon successful space negotiation and must be balanced with potential rate cost savings. Typical free merchandising to be negotiated includes the following:

- Free articles in the publication about your products or services
- Free literature digest placement
- Free buyer's guide listings
- Free white paper/case study publication
- Free direct mailings
- Free online ads
- Free link(s) from publication site to your site
- Free online listings
- Free Internet ads
- Free manufacturer's showcase ads
- Free bonus ads

Once negotiations are complete and contracts are approved, it is the buyer's responsibility to maintain contact with each publication to ensure they perform as expected. In addition to checking tear sheets and reviewing ad placement, the media buyer must follow up with the media to ensure that all merchandising programs are fulfilled and implemented (if required).

Measurement of Performance

Finally, the relative effects of the media placement are measured. Measurement techniques include the following tactics (reviewed during the discovery phase) as well as any custom techniques specific to your company or a selected industry:

- Publication reader studies
- Sales force feedback
- Lead generation via response cards and other publication tools
- Lead conversion (how many leads are successfully converted to sales)
- Cost per lead
- Cost of fulfillment
- Sales cycle (audience measurement)
- Cost per sale (audience measurement)
- Sales pricing elasticity by target market (audience measurement)
- Any specific sales system data requirements

Sample Media Budget

A media budget provides a snapshot of a total media plan. Figure 6.1 illustrates a media budget for a company that is targeting four distinct marketplaces: education, health care, retail, and parks and recreation. Each of these markets is business to business, and each utilizes the company's products and services in different ways.

Based on the company's sales records and industry research, its primary selling seasons are March through May and August through October. Therefore, the majority of the media will appear during the buying season—or will begin 1 month in advance of the buying season and continue through that period in order to capture the most sales. "Fish when the fish are biting" is an old axiom in the marketing field. In other words, we cannot force customers to buy. We must wait until the customer is ready to buy and then make sure our message reaches them at the appropriate time.

Some publications also offer special editions targeting a specific product or service area. Although special interest editions should be analyzed individually to determine their value to the company, they can be an excellent way to advertise to prospective and existing customers, in that the subject matter of the publication is directly related to the products and services being sold. In this example, special interest editions are the only media placed outside the company's primary selling season.

Beginning on the left side of the spreadsheet, there are notations regarding each publication's metrics, including the following:

- Circulation
- CPM (cost per thousand readers)
- Target circulation (how many of the readers are part of the company's target audience)
- Target CPM
- Number of ads placed
- Total impressions generated
- Cost per publication

All this information was obtained from the publication's BPA statement. Most reputable publications are audited by the BPA and an annual statement is produced. This statement, which is readily available from the publication, provides a wealth of information about the publication's audience.

In this example, the BPA statement was telling. One might think the magazine with the largest circulation and the lowest CPM would be the most efficient purchase. Take a look at the gross circulation and CPM of the magazines listed under Education. You see that Pub 1 has the largest circulation of the group (96,845) with the lowest CPM ($63). Based on these facts alone, you might decide that Pub 1 is the most efficient media purchase. But when you isolate the actual target market by using the job titles and other information in the BPA statement, you find that although Pub 1 is an attractive media choice, Pub 4 offers the lowest target CPM ($71). Based on this information, more ads were purchased in Pub 4, as it most effectively reaches the targeted audience.

Of course, there are many factors in selecting media, as previously discussed. This is just one of the analytic tools that can be used to quantify the potential effectiveness of a specific medium.

At times, not all the desired information is available. For example, Pub 3 is not audited by the BPA. It is a smaller publication with a readership of only 4,500. This publication, however, is well known in the industry and has produced sales leads in the past. Based on experience, the company purchased space in this magazine, knowing that all the results would be tracked and reviewed in anticipation of creating next year's budget.

The sample budget also lists the total impressions generated by each publication to offer an overall idea of the impact the campaign might have in the marketplace, which is helpful in weighting budgets among various industries or media segments. The "1/2P4C" notations in the budget indicate ad size and color, in this case "one-half page, four-color." This allows the budget to be a "one look" item, showing all timing, costs, and production needs.

The Internet

The Internet is a wonderful medium—but it is not the marketing panacea many think it is. It is just another medium—no more, no less. In terms of marketing your Internet site, most successful Internet marketers have been successful because of their non-Internet promotion.

There needs to be a proper balance between online and offline marketing. Simply creating a site will do little or nothing for a business. You must drive potential customers to that site using search engine optimization as well as non-Internet media. You also must give your prospect a reason to visit your site—whether it is a contest, a special sales promotion, or interesting and useful information.

Google, Yahoo, and many others offer sponsored links and searches. These produce results for some, but *not* for the majority of advertisers. Check the prices carefully before you commit and then always perform a quick math check to see how many units you would have to sell in order to break even.

Facebook, Twitter, and other social media are the same. There is nothing wrong with the medium—but you must use it carefully and make sure it targets your audience. The use of social media is very time consuming, and you must be sure there is a return on your time investment. Social media requires *daily* activity in order to work, as does blogging.

And finally, always test before you commit. You may waste some money, but you will learn which media will work for your product or service.

Other Promotional Tools

Sales Promotions

Sales promotions are similar to discounting, in that they will reduce short-term profitability in order to stimulate trial of a product or service. Instead of reducing the price of the product or service, you use part of the potential profit to add value to the product or service in other ways. Used in conjunction with some form of promotional tool, such as direct mail in a business-to-business setting or consumer media in a retail situation, sales promotions give prospects a reason to visit your place of business or try your product or service.

For example, a fast food merchant may give free movie passes with the purchase of a specific meal. This type of joint promotion helps both the restaurant and the theater. Most important, the food establishment does not have to discount its primary product. Instead, it adds value to its product through the addition of a dissimilar but related entertainment product. If you cannot locate an appropriate cosponsor, you can purchase merchandise to use as part of the promotion.

Promotions take place in other settings as well. For instance, corporate and industrial buyers can "earn" trips or merchandise by increasing their annual purchases of specific products or services.

Many times, sales promotions tie in to a seasonal event or holiday. In fact, Secretary's Day and Grandparents Day were both invented by a national floral wire service to stimulate sending of flowers.

In addition to using promotions to stimulate the consumer to buy, promotions can stimulate your sales force to sell. Sales contests are effective tools for increasing profitability.

However, the same cautions that apply to price discounting apply to sales promotions. They should be short-term, seasonal events—not an ongoing circus of continual promotion. Used wisely, they can boost sales. Used continually, they will erode your profitability.

In-Store Promotions and Image Awareness

If you are a retailer, the way you arrange your store shelves and merchandise your products is a simple but very important part of promotion. For instance, successful grocers place children's cereals on low shelves and multigrain cereals on top. In the grocery business, shoppers make the majority (60% to 80%) of purchasing decisions in the store. Therefore, in-store displays, racks, shelf talkers, and signage are extremely important.

If you are in a business-to-business operation, your sales force, phone staff, and shipping department are the most visible parts of the operation. Train them well. Dress them up. A grumpy receptionist may be the only image a potential customer has of your company.

Public Relations

In principle, conducting local public relations is easy. It's as simple as making sure you send any news—whether it's a new employee, a change in location, acquisition of a new product line, change in store hours, or an award you won—to the appropriate media. In practice, however, it is easy to forget to send the information or to assume that all information is newsworthy.

Also, select the proper media for your public relations. Be wary of "ego PR." This is where you place more importance on the news announcements that stroke your ego than on those that will win you sales. For example, if you manufacture electrical conduits for use in heavy industry across the nation, it may be personally gratifying for the local newspaper to run a feature article about your company. Your neighbors will all comment and your family will be quite proud. Yet a similar article in a national trade publication would garner attention in the right place and would result in sales.

Of course, you should not refuse any opportunity. If, for instance, the local newspaper did run a story about your business, maximize its effect by sending copies of the story to all your customers and prospects. Do not miss any opportunity to communicate with your prospects and customers.

Direct Marketing

Direct marketing can be an excellent tool for closing the sale and for introducing a product line. As its name implies, this form of promotion is a direct link between the promoter and the buyer. Many people think of this as direct mail. Certainly, that is a large part of direct marketing, but it is just one technique. Direct marketing also incorporates inbound and outbound telemarketing, order fulfillment, suggestive selling, cross-selling, and many other techniques.

Direct Mail

Generally, a direct mail packet consists of the following:

- An outside carrier (such as an envelope)
- A letter
- A brochure
- A "lift" device
- A response device

If possible, a direct mail piece should be tested. However, most smaller businesses can't afford to test a direct mail piece. National companies consider a test to be as many as 10,000 pieces—more than some companies' total mailing.

When you cannot afford to test your mailings, there are some general ground rules for you to follow. Your first job as a marketer is to get the envelope opened. As a famous advertising executive once said, "You can't save souls in an empty church." To accomplish this, you must do five things.

First, select your target audience well and then personalize the envelope. It is also important that you use the person's correct title and spell their name correctly.

Second, use the level of postage that is most appropriate to your needs and budget. Do not fall into the trap of agonizing over the use of first-class versus bulk rates. However, metered mail will usually outperform stamped mail.

Third, when it is appropriate, print teaser copy on the outside of the envelope or package. Invite the recipient to open it. Tell them what they will gain by opening the package or what they will lose if they do not open the package. For example, doctors are extremely difficult to reach via direct mail. In order to make sure they would receive and open the envelope, one successful marketer printed "X-Ray Enclosed, Open Immediately" on the outside of the package. This virtually ensured that the doctor would receive and open the envelope. (Yes, there was an X-ray enclosed that was an integral part of the mailing.)

Fourth, when possible, send "dimensional" packages. It is hard to resist opening a box wrapped in brown paper or even a large fat envelope. One real estate developer went so far as to mail a promotional piece for an oceanfront property in a clear mailing tube, filled with a colorful brochure and a handful of white sand.

Last, identify your company on the outside of the package. You should be proud of your product and should not hesitate to place your company name and logo on the exterior of the envelope.

Once opened, the letter becomes the most important part of the mailing. Follow this quick formula when you write a direct mail letter:

- Offer the reader a benefit. If not in the first line, make sure you clearly state the benefit in the first paragraph.

- Restate the benefit in expanded terms, telling the reader in more detail how your product or service will help them.
- Reinforce all your claims with proof, evidence, testimonials, facts, or examples.
- Stress immediacy. Emphasize what the reader will lose if they do not act now.
- Use a strong closing statement that emphasizes action.
- Include a postscript. Researchers have found that a P.S. is often the most read portion of a selling letter. Make sure your P.S. is strong and meaningful.

As for the format of the letter, many direct mail firms have found that the following formats work best:

- A two- to four-page letter will perform better than a single-page letter. (Four-page letters are usually 11" × 17" sheets, folded once.)
- Keep the look of your letters friendly. Use indented paragraphs and ragged right margins. Do not crowd the margins or use single spacing. Remember, your goal is to make it easy for the reader to absorb your selling message.
- You can also direct the attention of your readers to important parts of your letter with underlining or the use of a second color to emphasize important benefits. However, use this technique sparingly—it loses its effectiveness if overdone.
- Include a brochure, flyer, or circular. This piece should use a combination of art and photography to illustrate key selling features. If the item you are promoting is expensive, you should also consider the use of color photographs—the additional cost will result in additional sales and is worth the expense.
- In addition to the letter and brochure, the recipient needs to be able to respond easily to your offer. Include a response card or envelope and also display your phone number prominently. In addition, busy-looking reply cards printed in colored ink or on colored paper will generate more response

than clean-looking cards or order forms printed in black and white.

- And finally, include a "lift letter"—so named because it will "lift" the response to your mailer. In its simplest form, the lift letter is a small note card, with the message "Read Only If You Don't Plan to Buy . . ." printed on the outside. On the inside, there is a last plea to try to change your mind. In a more sophisticated form, the lift letter is a separate printed piece that uses a powerful closing argument, either negative or positive, to incite action on the part of a reader. The lift letter emphasizes what you will gain or lose in a dramatic way. It is sometimes a bit outlandish in its approach because it is a final effort to incite action. Properly constructed, it will do just that—resulting in sales for you.

If you can afford to test your mailing, follow these simple rules.

- Test only a single item at a time. For example, if you have done previous mailings, do not change both the price and the selling message in a test mailer. If you do, you will not know which change is responsible for the results.
- Carefully record all your test results.
- Keep copious records of when you received each response and note any demographic similarities or patterns.
- Do not overtest.
- If your direct mail program is producing positive results, do not change it.
- Whenever you can, ask your customers what they think about your mailing program. Do not make massive changes over a single person's response, though.

The Mailing List

Perhaps the most important single component of a direct mail campaign is the mailing list. After all, without a good list, you have no hope of achieving positive results.

There are many services that will rent you a list, many of whom will send you a free catalog. For a list of more than 600 mail list companies that will provide you with a catalog, send your check or money order for $2.00 to the following address:

> The Direct Marketing Association
> Great Catalogue Guide
> 6 E. 43rd Street
> New York, New York 10017

After the Mailing

In most businesses, it is appropriate to follow up mailings with tele-marketing. For instance, the best clothing sales representatives have an extensive customer list. They send a flyer to each person on their list and follow it up with a personal telephone call to inform them of the showing of a new line or of an upcoming sale.

Successful restaurateurs will visit each of the businesses in the area to post lunch menus on the bulletin boards and extend a personal invitation to visit the restaurant. They will then continue to stay in touch with the office manager by phone.

When dealing with a large target audience, telemarketers will use a set schedule and a script to follow up each mailing. They follow up on promotional offers as well as following up with existing customers. For example, a typical telemarketing staff (even if it is one person) might have the following responsibilities.

Follow-Up to Direct Mailings

Assume you have "flighted" your mailings so that you are sending out 5,000 pieces over a 13-week cycle. This would amount to about 385 pieces per week, or 77 per day. (Flighting is the process of segmenting your mailings into a delivery pattern—for example, sending out a mailing every 7 days. Each mailing is called a "flight.")

During week one, you would mail the 385 pieces, noting who would receive them. During week two, you would mail the second flight of 385 pieces and begin to call the 385 people to whom you mailed during week one. During week three, you would mail 385 additional pieces and begin to call those to whom you mailed during week two.

This pattern of mailing will allow you to manage your efforts and successfully conduct outbound telemarketing.

Response to Incoming Orders

Assuming your product mix is good and the mailings well handled, you will generate a response to your mailings—some of which will come to you by phone. You must be ready to answer these incoming calls and to accept orders. This is not just an opportunity to accept an order; it is an opportunity to cross-sell another product or upgrade the order by increasing the total purchase.

In order to do this successfully, you will need to train your operators in the art of suggestive selling and supply them with working scripts.

Customer Contact

You can also use outbound telemarketing to stay in contact with your customers. For example, if you are selling a product that you reorder frequently, you will want to maintain a list of customers who have ordered within a predetermined period. Say the average usage cycle for your product is 30 days. You will want to contact customers who have not reordered within 45 to 60 days to find out why they have not reordered. This will also require writing a set script or a list of questions for your telemarketers to ask. You may also wish to contact customers on a regular basis for PR purposes. This type of call can be used simply to make certain that your customers are satisfied and to probe for selling opportunities at the same time. This is also an excellent time to gain referral information from your customers or to gather information for future product testimonials.

The Sales Force

Most of us who started a business did so because we felt we were good at something. Very soon we found out that we became so busy doing that something, we did not have time for selling. Thus we could not grow. To counteract this, you have two broad choices. You can either hire a sales force or hire someone to assist you in managing your business while you go out and sell.

Before you make your decision, ask yourself several questions:

- Am I good at selling?
- Have I ever sold before?
- Is my hands-on expertise vital to the day-to-day survival of the company?
- Can I afford to hire additional staff?
- Do I have to sell my product or service in person or can it be sold via the mail or telephone?
- Do I require a national presence?
- Can I bundle my product or service with a compatible product or service to be promoted or sold by another company?

Your answers should help you determine if you need a sales force. If you do need a sales force, the answers will help you decide how they should sell. You may need to use personal calling, direct mail, telemarketing, or a combination of many methods. By answering these questions, you will also be able to clarify who should do the selling.

For instance, many fine artists find they are not well suited for sales. Therefore, they hire agents. The agents take care of all the business arrangements and the artists produce the art. In an alternator repair business, the roles might reverse. The owner could hire technicians to repair the equipment while he sold the service.

Once hired, part of an overall marketing plan should cover how to train, compensate, and motivate the sales force.

Suggestive Selling

Suggestive selling is an excellent way to increase sales by increasing the size or value of an order or by selling additional items in your product or service line.

The most effective way to put suggestive selling to use is by conducting short group training sessions. This allows time to ask real-life questions and provides time to demonstrate the selling techniques.

In general, these sessions should cover the basic techniques and closes used in suggestive selling and facilitate open discussions about how you can apply the techniques to your particular situation.

Suggestive Selling Techniques

Please note that these selling techniques apply to either personal selling or telemarketing.

- Smile. Be enthusiastic. If you are not excited about your product, how can you excite your customers? Telemarketers find that a real physical smile can be "heard" by the customer and will lead to increased sales.
- Listen to your customer. Probe to find the real meaning of what they are saying. You will gain valuable information to help you close the sale.
- Plan for the sale. Traditionally, there are *five steps* in the selling process:

  1. Determine the prospect's needs.
  2. Get the prospect to listen.
  3. Present the selling benefits.
  4. Anticipate/overcome objections.
  5. Close the sale.

In telemarketing, the use of a script or fact sheet facilitates many of these steps. However, since each presentation is different, the telemarketer must have a variety of closing techniques to use.

The Assumptive Close

In this close, you merely take for granted that the prospect is going to buy what you are offering. This is a very positive and effective close. Use it when your prospect seems receptive to the proposition.

- Example: How many (items) would you like?

- Example: The total order is (amount) including our new
  (item), which most of our customers are ordering. (This
  assumes you have already introduced the new item to them,
  but they did not indicate a preference for it.)

The Choice Close

Always give the prospect a choice. Never give the prospect an opportunity to answer "yes" or "no." State the item you really want to sell last in
the sequence. When the prospect has no real preference, the last item
mentioned is usually the one selected.

- Wrong: Would you like to buy a (item)?
- Right: Would you like a (item) in our 6-pack or our more
  economical 30-pack?

The Action Close

Use this close when the prospect appears interested but is having trouble making up his mind. In telemarketing, this close is assumptive in
nature but is based on an action that you will take, such as filling out
the order form.

- Example: Would you like to charge this to your Visa or
  MasterCard?
- Example: Would you like to make an appointment for Tuesday
  or Thursday?

Maintain Your Focus

Your primary objective is simple: to sell products. If a prospect begins to
stray from the subject by offering complaints about the company, asking about upcoming trade shows, or any subject other than the one you
called about, steer the prospect back to the topic at hand.

1. Listen to what they have to say.
2. Respond to it quickly and efficiently.

3. Use it to steer the prospect back to the subject at hand.

Used properly, many businesses have found that suggestive selling can increase their sales by up to 25%.

Creative Materials

No matter what media elements you select or printed pieces you have to produce, you will need to fill the time or space with copy or creative elements. There is a simple rule for judging creative concepts and materials, which will apply whether you choose to hire a professional advertising agency or do the work yourself: "It's not creative unless it sells."

This is an often-used quote by David Ogilvy, one of the world's renowned leaders in the field of advertising. Quite simply, it is easy for us to produce "creative for creative's sake." A cute headline amuses us—even if it obscures the message. Alternatively, we want our ads and brochures to be more beautiful than functional. As for copy, Ogilvy offers us the following guidelines:

David Ogilvy's Seven Rules for Headlines

1. Headlines should appeal to the reader's self-interest by promising a benefit.
2. Inject the maximum news into the headline. Products, like people, are most interesting when they are first born.
3. Include the brand name in the headline.
4. Write headlines that will induce the reader to read the subhead and the body copy. You cannot save souls in an empty church.
5. Write headlines that will sell. Do not worry about the length. Twelve-word headlines get almost as much readership as three-word headlines.
6. Do not use a headline that requires readership of body copy to make it comprehensible.
7. Never use tricky or irrelevant headlines. Do not try to be clever. People read too fast to figure out what you are trying to say.

Selecting the proper methods and content is important. However, the most important portion is the heart of the plan—your strategies.

In Summary

There are many tools available to help you market your company. No single tool will be best and not all tools work for all companies.

1. All media or tools should be researched and measured (tracked) continually.
2. Initial research should be conducted to match the media or tool with your product or service. Not all tools work for all people. This research should result in a "cost per" metric that is appropriate to the tool or medium. Always remember that the metric must apply to your audience segment, not the total audience.
3. Monitoring or tracking must be employed to obtain a cost-per-sale metric.
4. Cull poorly performing media and invest more in positively performing media.
5. Media sales representatives are not consultants. They do not have your interest at heart. Their only goal is to sell you their media. You must keep that in mind when purchasing any marketing tool.

CHAPTER 7

A Working Model

Before you begin to develop specific goals, strategies, and tactics, take the time to review your work in this manual. You may wish to remove and consolidate your completed worksheets, including the following:

- Marketing Matrix
- "Benefits Package"
- Market Segmentation Matrix
- Competitive Analysis
- Trends Analysis
- Mission Statement

Now, with that information in mind, list four goals your marketing plan will achieve and rank them in order of priority. You may be most comfortable working with the broadest goal first. For instance, if you have a new business, your first goal would be to introduce your company to your target audience. Your other goals would be more specific, such as achieving certain levels of market share and reaching a sales goal in an allotted period.

1. _____
2. _____
3. _____
4. _____

Developing Strategies and Tactics

Now, with the four Ps in mind (price, product, place, and promotion), list the strategies and tactics you will use to fulfill each goal. Remember, strategies are directional in nature; tactics are specific tools such as in-store promotions, types of advertising, sales promotions, and so forth.

Be specific. The tactics you list will form the basis for your working budgets. For instance, if one of the goals you previously listed was to make 1,000 sales in the first 6 months, your strategy might be to focus on a specific product or service benefit that is unique to your company. The tactics could include advertising media, trade shows, and public relations.

Goal #1: _____

    Strategies:

        _____
        _____
        _____

    Tactics:

        _____
        _____
        _____

    Measurement: How will your measure your results?

        _____
        _____
        _____

Goal #2: _____

    Strategies:

        _____
        _____
        _____

    Tactics:

        _____
        _____
        _____

    Measurement: How will your measure your results?

        _____
        _____

Developing Working Budgets

By concentrating on goals, strategies, and tactics, you can effectively break a plan down into manageable portions. The same holds true of individual product plans. In fact, the umbrella marketing plan is usually the framework for many smaller plans dealing with product lines or individual target markets.

After you have developed your goals, strategies, and tactics, you will need to assemble working budgets, based on a 12-month calendar, with supporting budgets for each major component.

You can determine the size of your budget in several ways. Many companies use one or a combination of the following elements:

Percentage of Sales

This method allocates a particular amount based on gross sales. An example might be to allow a total of 4.5% for all advertising, with 3.0% for broadcast media, 0.5% for production, 0.5% for newspaper, and the remaining 0.5% for yellow pages.

Competition

Using this method, you simply look at what your competitors spend and use their expenditures as a guideline. This method is used in conjunction with one of the other methods and should not be used as a sole determining factor.

Achievement of Sales Goals

This method of budgeting is, perhaps, the most sophisticated and is used by organizations selling products to industry, since it ties directly to your sales goals and the relative cost of acquiring each sale.

However, this method requires a sales and marketing history and cannot be used during the first year of business. In essence, you must track the effectiveness of each budget element used in the past. You must know which budget item generated each sale. Thus you will know that public relations generated 100 sales and trade advertising (in specific publications) generated 500 sales. Then you look at the total cost of each to isolate the cost per sale. If you spent $3,000 in public relations and generated 100 sales, the cost per sale was $30. If you spent $10,000 on trade advertising and generated 500 sales, the cost per sale was $20. Then you prepare your budget based on this information, assigning a higher percentage of your budget to the categories that achieve the greatest number of sales at the lowest cost per sale. And finally, by comparing your sales goal to the cost per sale, you can determine the necessary level of spending. If your goal is 1,000 sales and the average cost per sale is $220, your total budget should be approximately $220,000 for the year.

In Summary

In this chapter, you have learned how to create broad goals for your marketing plan and how to create strategies, tactics, and measurement processes. You also learned how to create a working budget and how to establish measurement criteria for your spending.

These elements work together to form your working model—or the nuts and bolts that you'll use to implement your plan.

CHAPTER 8

Bringing the Total Plan Together

In working through this manual, you have developed pieces of information. You have researched your marketplace, developed a competitive analysis, written a mission statement, and listed goals, strategies, and tactics. Your final task was to produce a working budget.

Separately, these elements are nothing more than bits of information. Together, they will form the basis for an ongoing marketing effort.

The successful marketer will now take these separate elements and build a marketing handbook. The working forms you have completed in this manual will comprise the section headers of your handbook, allowing you to add pertinent information as needed, updating it with new information and modifying it as the marketplace changes. In short, this handbook will become the informational core of your marketing plan.

The last step in the creation of your plan is to review it to make certain you are in agreement with every facet. Once you've done that, it's time to construct and implement an action plan.

An action plan is composed of a series of action steps with scheduled beginning and ending times. You will need an overall action plan for each of your major goals. Within each of those action plans will be a number of action steps. For example, your first step might be outlining the materials you will need to produce (flyers, ads, sales training outlines, etc.) for each action plan. In this outline, you would list the necessary items as well as the deadline for the development of each.

Next, you isolate the action steps for each of these elements. For instance, if you are going to develop a brochure, the first action step is to outline the contents of the brochure. Then you design the layout, create the copy, and obtain art and printing estimates. The purpose of listing specific action steps with specific deadlines is to make sure that you can complete the project in a timely manner and that you don't get the proverbial "cart before the horse." In essence, the action plans and their individual steps will form a road map for the successful execution of your plan.

It's Up to You!

In order to manage a marketing plan, you must make an ongoing commitment to evaluate and update the plan. Here is a look at some of the responsibilities of a marketing manager:

- *Allocating resources.* You will always have a limited source of resources—both financial and staff. Therefore, it is your duty to select areas in which your company will compete and the extent to which you will compete.
- *Ensuring that your company is fishing where the fish are biting.* As simple as it sounds, you must carefully select your specific market area and then concentrate your efforts in that area. It is extremely easy to scatter your resources across a number of target markets and dilute the effect.
- *Making an offer they can't refuse.* Remember the four Ps. Keep them in mind. The total package you offer your prospects will determine your ultimate success or failure. You must design a marketing mix that will highlight your benefits and will add value for the customer.

What Makes You Different?

Think of your own buying patterns. You purchase certain goods or services because you believe they are different in some way from their competitors. In order to compete effectively, not only will you have to identify your differential advantage, but you will also have to strive continually to update it.

Make Your Plan Part of the Corporate Culture

Many excellent marketing plans are quietly gathering dust on a shelf. They may be reviewed and updated once a year, but they are never really put into action. It is your duty to put the plan in action. Make it work— every day.

Conclusion

A successful company will use a part of each of the methods presented in *Strategic Marketing Planning for the Small to Medium-Sized Business* to create a marketing budget.

Figure 6.1 provides a sample of such a budget, illustrating a campaign designed to sell a service to a specific industry. After analyzing the target market and the competition and reviewing its goals and strategies, the company selected trade publication advertising, trade public relations, flighted direct mail, and attendance at trade shows as primary promotional tactics.

Once you have developed a working budget, it is important to review each tactic in light of its overall weight or importance to the campaign. For instance, if the tactic on which you will spend the most money is garnering you the least amount of sales, then perhaps you should reallocate the dollars. Make sure each budget dollar you list will contribute its fair share to your bottom-line profits.

How to Eat an Elephant

You will be rewarded handsomely if you put in the time and effort to develop a well-thought-out marketing plan. Your sales will grow and your business will prosper. However, remember that you must base your plan on fact, not opinion, and you must take the time to develop and test each phase of the plan carefully before you implement it.

You develop a good marketing plan in the same way you would eat an elephant—"one bite at a time."

Index

Announcing the Business Expert Press Digital Library

Concise E-books Business Students
Need for Classroom and Research

This book can also be purchased in an e-book collection by your library as

- a one-time purchase,
- that is owned forever,
- allows for simultaneous readers,
- has no restrictions on printing,
- can be downloaded as PDFs from within the library community.

Our digital library collections are a great solution to beat the rising cost of textbooks. E-books can be loaded into their course management systems or onto students' e-book readers.

The **Business Expert Press** digital libraries are very affordable, with no obligation to buy in future years.

For more information, please visit **www.businessexpertpress.com/librarians**. To set up a trial in the United States, please contact **Sheri Dean** at sheri.dean@globalepress.com; for all other regions, contact **Nicole Lee** at nicole.lee@igroupnet.com.

OTHER TITLES IN OUR MARKETING STRATEGY COLLECTION
Collection Editor: **Naresh Malhotra**

- *Building a Marketing Plan: A Complete Guide* by Ho Yin Wong, Kylie Radel, and Roshnee Ramsaran-Fowdar
- *Conscious Branding* by David Funk and Anne Marie Levis
- *Decision Equity: The Ultimate Metric to Connect Marketing Actions to Profits* by Piyush Kumar and Kunal Gupta
- *Developing Winning Brand Strategies* by Lars Finskud
- *Marketing Strategy in Play: Questioning to Create Difference* by Mark Hill
- *Top Market Strategy: Applying the 80/20 Rule* by Elizabeth Rush Kruger

CPSIA information can be obtained at www.ICGtesting.com
Printed in the USA
BVOW010652151212

308012BV00007B/152/P